FORTRESS
Introduction to
Black Church History

FORTRESS
Introduction to
Black Church History

Anne H. Pinn
Anthony B. Pinn

Fortress Press ◆ Minneapolis

To Mrs. Sarah Bexley
and
the unnamed ancestors

◆

FORTRESS INTRODUCTION TO BLACK CHURCH HISTORY

Copyright © 2002 Augsburg Fortress. All rights reserved. Except for brief quotations in critical articles or reviews, no part of this book may be reproduced in any manner without prior written permission from the publisher. Write: Permissions, Augsburg Fortress, Box 1209, Minneapolis, MN 55440.

Scripture quotations are from the Revised Standard Version of the Bible, © 1946, 1952, 1971 by the Division of Christian Education of the National Council of the Churches of Christ in the USA. Used by permission.

Cover illustrations: Barbara Zuber, *Graphics for Worship 2.0,* Copyright © 1999 Augsburg Fortress. Used by permission.

Library of Congress Cataloging-in-Publication Data
Pinn, Anne H.
   Fortress Introduction to Black church history / Anne H. Pinn and Anthony B. Pinn.
   p. cm.
   Includes bibliographical references and index.
   ISBN 0-8006-3442-X (alk. paper)
   1. African American churches—History. 2. African Americans—Religion.
   I. Title: Introduction to Black church history. II. Pinn, Anthony B. III. Title.

BR563.N4 P48 2001
277.3'0089'96073—dc21   2001051067

The paper used in this publication meets the minimum requirements of American National Standard for Information Sciences — Permanence of Paper for Printed Library Materials, ANSI Z329.48-1984.

Manufactured in the U.S.A.   AF 1-3442
05   04   03   02   1   2   3   4   5   6   7   8   9   10

CONTENTS

102228

PREFACE

Obscure in origin, secret in development, rich and complex in its flowering, the oldest and most influential institution in African American life remains the Black Church. In fact, the African American engagement with Christianity has not only shaped, consoled, and empowered a people caught in slavery for more than two centuries, it has also captured and emboldened their spirit in such a way as to engender profound social change across all of America.

What has inspired and enabled this movement? How has it interacted with white Christianity and with other elements in American life? Who were its chief prophets and lights? How have its roots shaped its present social agenda? Where is it headed? To answer these questions, this little volume traces the story, the spirit, the ideas, and the activities of African American Christianity, especially in its inception as a slave religion and its development after the Civil War in seven of the largest denominational bodies.

As Americans come to appreciate the crucial role of African American Christianity in our society, and as black people themselves become more curious about their religious roots, we hope this book can help. It sketches the main historical turns of the Black Church, profiles prominent historical figures, and gives the reader a sense of the underlying commitments, community life, and contests that animate these traditions. As an introduction, penned by a clergywoman and an academic, our survey relies on and disseminates the more technical and in-depth work of others.

Further, African American Christianity is also richly diverse and constantly evolving. There is no monolithic Black Church. The movements and church bodies whose stories we tell in this volume— mainly Methodist, Baptist, and Pentecostal—are carriers of some of the main traditions, but there are many others, including African American Catholicism, blacks in the United Methodist Church, and blacks in a host of other Pentecostal traditions. Our brief survey can offer only a sampling of the varieties of African American church life, which we hope the reader will pursue through the many Study Questions, Suggested Readings, and Websites we note at the ends of discussions. We sincerely hope that readers—churched and unchurched, students and lay people, African Americans and others—will find here an invitation to deeper probes into African American Christian life and thought.

◆

Although the authors alone are responsible for flaws within this text, the successful completion of the volume was made possible by the kind assistance of many individuals. We would like to begin by thanking Michael West, our editor at Fortress Press, whose commitment to the project was inspiring, and Zan Ceeley, whose work as production editor for this project was detailed and insightful. Special thanks must be given to Rev. Dr. John Ross Dixon, who provided books, articles, and encouragement. We are also grateful to Rev. Joseph D. Kerr, who took the time to talk and share his storehouse of knowledge. Mother Esther G. Clark has been a good friend and source of support for many years. The encouragement of Stephen Angell, Peter Paris, Katie Cannon, and numerous others must be acknowledged. Thank you. As always we are grateful to Raymond Pinn, Linda Bryant, and Joyce Pinn (Anne's children and Anthony's siblings) for their continued support and help. They have always believed that "we could." Special thanks also to Cheryl Johnson (Anthony's wife) for her patience.

The Making of Black Christians

With the growth in the population of enslaved Africans in North America during the 1600s came an increase in laws designed to tightly control the behavior of slaves. These laws made it clear that enslaved Africans were to be regarded as property for life and through all generations. Understanding themselves to be "civilized," Europeans reasoned that Africans must be uncivilized. In the words of an early Portuguese participant in the slave trade, Gomes Eannes De Azurara, Africans "lived like beasts, without any custom of reasonable beings—for they had no wine, and knowledge of bread or they were without the covering of clothes, or the lodgement of houses; and worse than all, they had no understanding of good, but only know how to live in bestial sloth."[1]

Holding cave for enslaved Africans in Ghana (photo by author)

This commonly held attitude helped Europeans justify the enslavement of Africans because Europeans did not consider themselves to be harming fellow human beings but merely capturing and working beasts of burden. This cultural chauvinism, however, was not justification enough for some slaveholders who considered themselves Christians. These colonists needed a more overt theological rationale, so they consulted scripture for additional support. One passage in particular about Noah and his son Ham from the Book of Genesis was used to justify slavery:

> Noah was the first tiller of the soil. He planted a vineyard; and he drank of the wine, and became drunk, and lay uncovered in his tent. And Ham, the father of Canaan, saw the nakedness of his father, and told his two brothers outside. . . . When Noah awoke from his wine and knew what his youngest son had done to him, he said, "*Cursed be Canaan; a slave of slaves shall he be to his brothers.*" (Gen. 9:20-22; 24-25, RSV, italics added)

Europeans understood the enslavement of Africans as an extension or fulfillment of this biblical mandate and continued to reap the social and economic benefits of the slave trade. This perceived biblical justification for slavery had other serious consequences since it helped determine popular views on the religious capabilities—or lack thereof—of Africans. In short, it was believed that Africans could not possibly appreciate or need Christianity. Even those who were not convinced by this particular argument questioned the capacity of Africans to comprehend the Christian faith. Furthermore, resistance to the evangelizing of slaves often centered on a fear that such efforts would result in Africans thinking of themselves as equal to their owners and thus lead to disobedience and defiance. Many colonists were concerned that the conversion of slaves could topple slavery's delicate hierarchy and precarious rationale.

Still, a number of colonists were indeed concerned with the religious needs of Africans. They saw slavery as an opportunity to bring Africans to a proper understanding of God's word; in this way, they added to the Kingdom of God by converting the lost. These colonists felt that Africans were capable of understanding the gospel, and that Africans possessed souls just as Europeans did. Furthermore, most of these evangelists felt that spiritual conversion of Africans would not disrupt the system of slavery. They believed that the acquaintance of Africans with the Christian faith would make for better slaves because Africans would understand their place in the divine plan and realize that obedience to God required obedience to human authority. Religion came to be a mechanism of social control, which was particularly important in the middle and southern colonies where Africans represented a larger, more vital work force.

Christianization of the Slaves

Northern Efforts

In the northern colonies, the Quakers made an effort to convert slaves and *end* slavery, through the work of leaders such as John Woolman and Benjamin Lay. Meanwhile, Puritans typically sought to convert slaves and *maintain* slavery. Although many New Englanders shared with other colonists an indifference toward the spiritual welfare of Africans, ministers like John Eliot and Cotton Mather were intent on the religious instruction of slaves. During the late 1600s, Eliot informed slave owners that he wanted to give weekly religious instruction to slaves, and, in 1693, Mather developed the Society of Negroes, through which Africans received religious instruction.

"Door of No Return" in Ghana, through which
enslaved Africans passed to be loaded onto ships (photo by author)

Many influential colonists such as Mather believed that God had placed Africans under the control of Europeans as part of a providential plan. It was an act of mercy, the argument went, to enslave the body and free the soul from damnation. The result of this kind of thinking was often a paternalistic attitude toward Africans couched in religious terms. In the words of Mather:

> It is come to pass by the providence of God, without which there comes nothing to pass, that poor Negroes are cast under your government and protection. You take them into your families; you look on them as part of your possession; and you expect from their service a support, and perhaps an increase, of your other possessions. How agreeable it would be if a religious master or mistress thus attended would not think with themselves, "Who can tell but that this poor creature may belong to the election of God! Who can tell but that God may have sent this poor creature into my hands so that one of the elect may by my means be called and by my instruction be made wise unto salvation. The glorious God will put an unspeakable glory upon me if it may be so!"[2]

Regardless of the intent, Bible-based religious communities made the conversion of Africans difficult with strict regulations concerning church membership. Unlike the conversion efforts of Catholics in the Americas, Protestants understood salvation to involve regeneration of the soul outwardly marked by radically new conduct. What form could this take for the slaves, who were a socially and culturally despised population, whose bondage limited their activities, and whose "teachers" had fundamental reservations concerning the equality of Africans with Europeans?

Few Africans received fellowship into Puritan churches. The dominant version of the Christian faith found in northern colonies required some access to the written word and thus some degree of education. Even if the slave system could survive the Christianizing of slaves, church services and instruction would result in lost labor time. Even worse, since only "heathens" could be enslaved, conversion of Africans would implicitly require Puritans and other slave holders to free them because Christians should not hold other Christians in bondage. Slaveholders faced a dilemma that pitted economic and social sensibilities against religion. To Christianize enslaved Africans could result in economic losses and social disorder. But failure to spread the gospel contradicted Jesus' calling of the redeemed to service: "Go therefore and make disciples of all nations, baptizing them in the name of the Father and of the Son and of the Holy Spirit, teaching them to observe all that I have commanded you; and lo, I am with you always, to the close of the age" (Matt. 28:19-20, RSV). Several colonies attempted to resolve problems related to the baptizing of slaves by passing laws arguing that baptism did not necessitate the release of slaves from bondage.

Southern Efforts

After 1702, the Society for the Propagation of the Gospel in Foreign Parts carried forward the early Protestant effort to convert slaves within the middle and southern colonies. This Anglican Church organization did not oppose slavery, and in fact several of its ministers were slaveholders. Although its leaders were quite clear in expressing the beneficial relationship between Christianizing Africans and the economics of slaveholding, the approach taken by the society met with some opposition because it entailed teaching slaves to read and write. It was believed that slaves who could read would also think and would develop a strong hatred for the system of slavery and thus threaten its sustainability. Chaos could follow.

Slaveholders attending slave services (Courtesy of Photographs and Prints Division, Schomburg Center for Research in Black Culture, The New York Public Library)

The hostility of slaveholders toward missions led to Anglican ministers addressing enslaved Africans primarily through heavily monitored Sunday sermons. Attempts to get slaveholders to take some responsibility for religious instruction were largely unsuccessful.[3] Some, however, did feel obliged to look after their slaves. This is shown in the treatment of two Africans in the charge of Ebenezer Taylor:

> Mrs. Haige and Mrs. Edwards, who came lately to this Plantation [South Carolina], have taken extra-ordinary pains to instruct a considerable number of Negroes, in the principles of the Christian Religion, and to reclaim and reform them. The wonderful success they met with, in about half a year's time, encouraged me to go and to examine those Negroes, about their Knowledge of Christianity; they declared to me their Faith in the chief articles of our Religion, which they sufficiently explained; they rehearsed by heart, very distinctly, the Creed, the Lord's Prayer, and Ten Commandments; fourteen of them give me so great satisfaction, and were so desirous to be baptized, that I thought it my duty to do it on the last Lord's Day.[4]

The above represents a minority perspective concerning religious instruction for slaves in Colonial America. Therefore, the colonies would not experience large-scale Christian conversion of Africans until the first Great Awakening sparked by the preaching of Jonathan Edwards and other early evangelists.

The Great Awakenings

First Awakening

Beginning in the 1730s and hitting its stride in the 1740s, the first Great Awakening sparked the interest of Europeans who acknowledged the urgency of religious reform. In part a response to the Calvinistic ethos that touched many colonies, the Great Awakening revolved around a type of conversion marked by fantastic spiritual breakthrough expressed in strong emotional terms. Evangelists such as George Whitfield offered a religious experience that differed greatly from the rather staid tradition of the Puritans and Anglicans. Their message was full of vivid imagery of the pain and suffering sinners would endure if they did not surrender to the will of God. These evangelists preached that the world suffered because of the sinful ways of humans. God, they argued, would not allow evil to go unpunished forever. Therefore, they preached that energetic conversion was the only remedy for human sinfulness.

Although many denominations participated in this religious fervor, Baptists and Methodists dominated the revival field, particularly in the South. Baptist and Methodist evangelists spread this revival fire and brought both the free and the bound into the "Christian fold." Fiery sermons also pricked the consciences of slaveholders, who became increasingly concerned with their own salvation and the spiritual welfare of those around them, which had a significant impact on the Christianization of Africans. Historian Albert Raboteau reports that Methodist records show a growth in African membership of almost ten thousand between 1786 (when membership records were first distinguished by race) and 1790. Although less diligent with record keeping, Baptist churches showed an African membership of about twenty thousand.[5]

The success of Baptist and Methodist evangelists in gaining converts was due to a variety of factors. First, these ministers were free to conduct services in ways unknown to Puritan and Anglican ministers. Their relative freedom to address the particular issues and attitudes of the South also translated into a sense of spiritual individualism that allowed enslaved Africans and slaveholders to think beyond the confines of Anglican and Puritan precepts and institutions. For example, the teachings of the Great Awakening revivalists did not emphasize reading the catechism and other forms of religious training. Consequently, inner commitment and first-hand experience supplanted literacy as the prerequisite for conversion and spiritual renewal. According to Raboteau,

> While the Anglican clergyman tended to be didactic and moralistic, the Methodist or Baptist exhorter visualized and personalized the drama of sin and salvation, of damnation and election. The Anglican usually taught the slaves the Ten Commandments, the Apostles' Creed and the Lord's Prayer; the revivalist preacher helped them to feel the weight of sin, to imagine the threats of Hell, and to accept Christ as their only Savior. The enthusiasm of the camp meeting, as excessive as it seemed to some churchmen, was triggered by the personal, emotional appeal of the preacher and supported by the common response of members of his congregation.[6]

The importance of the felt presence of the Holy Spirit through shouting and possession harkened to a similar importance placed on spirit possession in West African religious practices. Beyond this, the practices of Methodists and particularly Baptists easily meshed with the practices of traditional African spirituality because they called attention to the importance of water. Enslaved Africans found Methodist and Baptist services appealing because the emphasis on the sacrament of baptism reflected the water rituals and "cults" many Africans had practiced in their homeland. In this sense, evangelistic Christianity served to link an African past with a North American present.[7]

In addition to some natural harmony with African sensibilities, the Great Awakening's theological ethos appealed to Africans because of its reliance on a "priesthood of all believers" mentality. Anyone who was saved and felt a calling to preach could do so. Because preaching the gospel was not limited to those with formal training, this allowed enslaved Africans to assume a role seldom held before this period. Throughout the geographic areas touched by the Great Awakening, and in areas without restrictions concerning black preachers, those of African descent, such as Harry Hoosier (often referred to as "Black Harry"), proclaimed the gospel. Both lay and ordained black ministers mark the development of new religious possibilities. However, the slave system was still in place, and even the new-found religious "freedoms" of Africans had to be circumscribed.

Second Awakening

This first Great Awakening was followed by a second awakening, which began about 1800. During this second awakening, the number of Africans converted increased as evangelists fought hard to establish themselves on plantations. Although the Baptist and Methodist churches gained the most converts, one of the major figures in the development of plantation missions was a Presbyterian minister, Charles Colcock Jones. Recognizing the inadequate gains made by the Christian churches among slaves from the late 1700s through the early 1800s, Jones argued for a much more sustained effort directly on the plantations. He was interested in extending the missionary efforts beyond select household slaves to all enslaved Africans. Appreciative of the groundwork laid by the Great Awakening, Jones argued that a systematic approach to Christianization meant moving beyond seasonal revivalism.

Plantation-based missions were particularly important because not all plantations were near churches, which made it difficult for both planters and enslaved Africans to attend services. Lectures, meetings, print media, and other organized methods helped spread the word about plantation missions, but these efforts met with some resistance because planters feared that mission activities were laced with an abolitionist agenda. Slaveholders had no interest in a gospel that sought to free both the body and the soul. As was the case earlier, missionaries made an effort to allay such worries by avowing a gospel that touched the soul and left social and economic arrangements intact.

Missionaries and evangelists provided religious instruction without exposing Africans to literacy in order to maintain the slave system and still preach the gospel. Another common practice was the instruction of slaves in the presence of slaveowners, who made certain the gospel did not stir rebellion—a fear that increased after well-known rebellions led by Nat Turner, Denmark Vesey, and Gabriel Prosser. Catechisms and other forms of instruction reinforced the master-slave relationship. According to one of the more popular texts, slaves were "to count their Masters 'worthy of all honour,' as those whom God has placed over them in this world; with all fear,' they are to be 'subject to them' and obey them in all things, possible and lawful, with good will and endeavour to please them well, . . . and let Servants serve their masters as faithfully behind their backs as before their faces. God is present to see, if their masters are not.[8]

Protestant churches increased their numbers through the plantation missions. According to some estimates, Methodism increased its African membership from roughly 118,000 to over 200,000 in the fifteen years between 1846 and 1861. During the same period, Baptist churches started with roughly 200,000 Africans and gained an additional 200,000.[9] But these were small numbers when compared to the roughly 4.5 million Africans in the United States by 1860.[10] When mindful of these millions of Africans in the United States, a question must be asked: What kinds of religion were these unconverted Africans practicing?

The Response of Africans to Christianization

Rejection of the Christian Faith

Not all those of African descent, whether free or bound, responded to this Christianizing process in the same way. For some, the only response to the hardships of enslavement was to reject all traditional Christian forms of religious practice and to embrace atheism or agnosticism.[11] Some of the secular songs of the time suggest how a number of enslaved Africans made light of Christian doctrine and committed themselves to securing their own welfare outside of talk about God. In fact, this perspective has been expressed throughout the centuries in the work songs and hollers that grew into the blues. During the period of enslavement, many Africans would have agreed with blues performer "Funny Paper" Smith. With a touch of sarcasm, Smith says:

> This must be the Devil I'm serving
> I know it can't be Jesus Christ
> 'Cause I asked him to save me
> and look like he's trying to take my life.[12]

Daniel Alexander Payne of the African Methodist Episcopal Church noted in 1839 with some worry that he had encountered enslaved Africans who denied the existence of God and frowned upon the Christian faith:

> The slaves are sensible of the oppression exercised by their masters'
> and they see these masters on the Lord's day worshipping in his holy
> Sanctuary. They hear their masters professing Christianity; they see
> these masters preaching the gospel; they hear these masters praying in
> their families, and they know that oppression and slavery are inconsis-
> tent with the Christian religion; therefore they scoff at religion itself—
> mock their masters, and distrust both the goodness and justice of God.
> Yes, I have known them even to question his existence.[13]

African Religions in North America

A number of Africans did not reject the Christian faith, rather they combined it with traditional African practices and developed religions that greatly resembled belief systems such as Vodou (Haiti),

Santería (Cuba), Obeah (Jamaica), or Shango (Trinidad). In the United States such practices are commonly referred to as *voodoo, conjure,* or *hoodoo.* The existence of alternative religious practices is evident in a variety of forms. Historian Yvonne Chireau points to such evidence in advertisements:

> In the latter part of the eighteenth century, there are further, scattered hints indicating the presence of supernatural traditions among Black bondspersons in the South. A 1784 advertisement of a runaway female slave in Savannah, Georgia, for example, suggests that not only did popular interest in clairvoyance, divination, and fortune-telling circulate widely among whites and African Americans, but to some extent such ideas functioned as marketable goods for resourceful Black bondspersons: 'Runaway from the subscriber, an elderly Negro woman named Luce, of a thin visage, and rather a small stature. . . . She . . . pretends to be skill[ed] in fortunetelling, by cutting of cards, whereby she imposes on young people.[14]

Scholars are uncertain how many Africans held such beliefs. It is also unknown how many slaves were Muslim. Allen Austin, a prominent scholar in the field of African American Islam, argues that somewhere between 15 and 25 percent of the early slaves were Muslims.[15] Although Austin's estimate may be high, written records do point to the presence of practicing Muslims during the antebellum period. As historian C. Eric Lincoln remarks, "The Africans were here with Islam before the founding of the Republic, and although the free expression of their religion was prohibited and suppressed during three centuries of servitude, the fire of the faith was never quite snuffed out. It survived in legends and tales, in memories and anecdotes, in unexplained urgencies challenging the terrible aridity of consciousness bracketing the endless centuries of servitude."[16]

Africanization of Christianity

Africans who embraced Christianity did so on their own terms, making it a unique expression of their questions and hopes, while rejecting versions of the gospel that appeared to justify slavery. Using their cultural memory of African practices, European notions of the Christian faith, and reflections on the hardships of their enslavement in North America, Africans produced their own unique form of

Christian expression. This new version of the Christian faith spoke to spiritual and physical freedom and opposed all faiths that denied the interconnectedness of these two freedoms. As Frederick Douglass notes in his autobiography, many slaves made an important distinction between the true gospel of Christ and the teachings of planters and plantation missionaries:

> What I have said respecting and against religion, I mean strictly to apply to the slaveholding religion of this land, and with no possible reference to Christianity proper; for, between the Christianity of this land, and the Christianity of Christ, I recognize the widest possible difference—so wide, that to receive the one as good, pure, and holy, is of necessity to reject the other as bad, corrupt, and wicked. . . . Indeed, I can see no reason, but the most deceitful one, for calling the religion of this land Christianity. I look upon it as the climax of all misnomers, the boldest of all frauds, and the grossest of all libels. Never was there a clearer case of "stealing the livery of the court of heaven to serve the devil in." I am filled with unutterable loathing when I contemplate the religious pomp and show, together with the horrible inconsistencies, which every where surround me. We have men-stealers for ministers, women-whippers for missionaries, and cradle-plunderers for church members. The man who wields the blood-clotted cowskin during the week fills the pulpit on Sunday, and claims to be a minister of the meek and lowly Jesus.[17]

Enslaved Africans recognized the contradiction between word and deed, and those who still embraced the Christian tradition moved beyond falsehoods and hypocrisy. They made the Gospel of Christ a liberating religious experience by dropping the message of docility and instead understanding the Christian life as a free existence. Those enslaved Africans who sought to shape the Christian faith in ways that responded to their existential condition and spiritual needs developed what is known as the *invisible institution*.

The invisible institution refers to secret religious meetings held by enslaved Africans, during which they forged a Christian tradition that responded more appropriately to their concerns and condition. Considered conspiratorial by planters, these meetings were illegal and could result in severe punishment. Because the content of Christian services that were sponsored by slaveholders simply buttressed the system of slavery, enslaved Africans met secretly in secluded locations—*hush harbors*—to hear sermons and sing songs that better addressed their condition. When meetings could not be held in private locations, other mechanisms were used to maintain secrecy, including praying into containers of water to muffle the sound. Although the secret nature of these meetings explains the limited documentary evidence, collections of interviews with former slaves give some sense of what these meetings entailed.

Frederick Douglass
(Courtesy of Clements Library, University of Michigan)

In keeping with the Great Awakenings, these meetings were known to be energetic, with participants "catching the spirit" and shouting praises to God. According to the following account: "An' den de black folks 'ud git off, down in de crick bottom, er in a thick'et, an' sing an' shout an' pray. Don't know why, but de w'ite folks sho' didn't like dem ring shoults de cullud folks had. De folks git in er ring an' sing an' dance, an' shout; de dance is jes; a kinder shuffle, den hit gits faster, an' faster as dey gits wa'amed up; an' dey moans an' shouts; an' sings, an' claps, an' dance. Some ob em gits 'zuasted an' dey drop out, an' de ring gits closer. Sometimes dey sing an' shout all night. . . ."[18] The tone and intent of these meetings did not revolve simply around spiritual happiness. Hush harbor meetings also served as an opportunity to link religious development and physical freedom. Africans understood that faithful service to God and proper treatment of others would result in liberation from slavery. In the words of one former slave,

> We used to slip off in de woods in de old slave days on Sunday evening way down in de swamps to sing and pray to our own liking. We prayed for dis day of freedom. We come from four and five miles away to pray together to God dat if we don't live to see it, do please let our chillun live to see a better day and be free, so dat dey can give honest and fair service to de Lord and all mankind everywhere.[19]

Camp meeting in the South (Courtesy of Photographs and Prints Division,
Schomburg Center for Research in Black Culture, The New York Public Library)

Christianity, as developed by enslaved Africans and their descendants, contained a code of ethics and morality that shaped communal interaction and personal conduct. For example, conversion often required a rejection of worldly activities, such as dancing, drinking, and playing of certain types of music. It was understood that a Christian life required discipline and self-denial, and a recognized conversion experience was preceded by a long period of remorse over the sinfulness of one's life. However, maintaining a sense of community that nurtured converts was extremely difficult because churches run by slaveholders did not allow for much spiritual companionship. Yet there is evidence that some independent black churches existed as early as the 1700s in the South.

These black churches represented a blend of African and European worldviews and religious sensibilities that formed a unique expression of the Christian faith. In these churches, black Christians forged a spiritual space in which to think through the Gospel of Christ in light of their particular needs. Often, just finding the physical space for this reflection was a task that required careful attention. According to one early church leader, "in the latter part of the eighteenth century, colored people sought a secluded spot for their churches. In a back alley; behind the woods; where they could sing and pray late and loud without disturbing the 'white folks.'"[20] Within these spaces, black churches grew and gave expression to beliefs, desires, and goals of both the free and enslaved. They expressed, in fuller form, the nascent religious sensibilities and ritual structures forged during hush harbor meetings. Within these churches African Americans worked out their relationship with the Christian God and also fought for full participation in American society.

By 1936, the Black Church represented by the major seven denominations included over thirty thousand church buildings, mostly in rural areas, and a membership of roughly five million, concentrated in urban areas.[21] By 1970, the Black Church grew to include more than 10 million black Christians in the United States alone and hundreds of thousands of members abroad. To accommodate its increasingly international makeup, the infrastructure became more layered, the hierarchy more complex, and its opinions more theologically diverse. The Black Church went through periods of relative silence on social issues, but, in other periods, it was a major force for civil rights. Throughout its existence, the Black Church remained *potentially* the most powerful organization in black communities. Many scholars, ministers, and laity alike try to capture this opinion of the church's influence by talking about the Black Church and black America as if they are synonymous. Joseph Washington, a scholar of black church history, drew upon biblical imagery from the Book of Genesis to make this point: "In the beginning was the black church, and the black church was with the black community, and the black church was the black community. The black church was in the beginning with the black people; all things were made through the black church, and without the black church was not anything made that was made. In the black church was life; and the life was the light of the black people."[22] Although Washington's statement is too sweeping, the programs and platforms adopted by the contemporary Black Church have their roots in the thought and action of earlier years, a time during which the position of the Black Church within the black community was somewhat secure.

The involvement of black churches in social activism has been the subject of many recent books, documentaries, and conversations. Few deny the impact that churches are having on the pressing issues facing the United States. Scholars such as James Cone, C. Eric Lincoln, and others have explored this central question: What in the church's thought and history promotes this social activism? While academics and students have benefited from the work of Cone, Lincoln, and other scholars of African American Religious Studies, little of this material finds its way into congregations or a more general audience outside the academy. As a result this disconnect between the academic discussion of the Black Church and the pews containing black Christian activists leads to various misunderstandings. For example, academics who study African American religion often write in ways that do not take into consideration the *actual* experience of black Christianity and other forms of African American religious expression. We suggest that those within churches do not always have a full understanding of the historical roots of their church's activism beyond general appeals to scriptural passages.

This book seeks to address the lack of knowledge about the historical roots of the Black Church and its activities with a brief history of the seven largest denominations, from their inception to the Civil Rights movement. The objective is to present the history of these denominations in a way that makes clear the interests and agendas of black churches from their early development to more recent years. We hope to help readers answer a central question: Why do African American churches have their current shape and concerns? Put another way, what about these churches made possible and likely their participation in the Civil Rights movement and post–Civil Rights activism? The time frame for this study is from 1750 until 1970, which captures the beginning of the Black Church tradition, the reformulation of the Black Church and its thought marked by the decline of the Civil Rights movement, and the growth of the Black Power movement.[23]

The book is divided into two sections. The first is concerned with the history of the seven largest black denominations. In addition to historical narratives, the discussion of each denomination includes a timeline, short biographical sketches, study questions, and a list of suggested reading. Furthermore, with respect to the logic behind these additional components, it must be noted that the possible figures for inclusion in the biographical sketches section number beyond what can be provided in a short introductory text. Recognizing this limitation, the authors have attempted to give readers only a sampling.[24] We believe the suggested reading lists give readers an opportunity to explore in greater depth the events and persons shaping each denomination discussed here. It should also be noted that the authors are aware of the millions of African American Christians located outside these seven denominations, who find homes in the Roman Catholic Church, the United Methodist Church, and so on. However, we limit our exploration to the seven largest denominations because by their numbers, an estimated 20–25 million combined, they represent the vast majority of the nation's African American Christians. In this way, attention to their development says something concerning the history of most African Americans Christians.

Following these brief historical sketches, the second section is more concerned with the theology that shaped and motivated the activities of black churches. The fourth chapter looks at the social gospel and black theology informing the institutional and intellectual development of black churches during the period highlighted by this book. The documentary appendix provides readers with two primary documents that highlight the tone and texture of the theological arguments and concerns found in both the social gospel and black theology. We believe that the perspective and information provided in this text are enhanced through the combination of our vocations. One is an academic with no formal allegiance to the church and the other is a committed Christian minister. We hope that our outside/insider perspective enhances the text and provides balance. We also hope that this book will help explain the value of black churches and inspire members of various black churches to take pride in their accomplishments and to look to the future. In the words of the song known to so many church members: "I don't feel no ways tired. I've come too far from where I started from."

Suggested Reading

Giddings, Paula. *When and Where I Enter: The Impact of Black Women on Race and Sex in America*. New York: Morrow, 1984. With sharp analysis and insightful historical presentation, this is essential reading for those interested in the impact of gender roles and stereotypes on the life of black women in America

MacRobert, Iain. *The Black Roots and White Racism of Early Pentecostalism in the U.S.A.* New York: St. Martin's, 1988. MacRobert provides a concise history of pentecostalism in the United States and places the quest for sanctification within the context of US racial relations during the late nineteenth century and early twentieth century.

Raboteau, Albert J. *Slave Religion: The Invisible Institution in the Antebellum South.* New York: Oxford University Press, 1978. Raboteau's discussion of the Christianizing of enslaved Africans and their subsequent transformation of the Christian faith into a unique expression of religious commitment is a classic. This continues to provide one of the best presentations of religion within African American communities prior to the twentieth century.

Richardson, Harry V. *Dark Salvation: The Story of Methodism as It Developed among Blacks in America.* Garden City, N.Y.: Doubleday, 1976. This important work discusses the appeal and adaptation of Methodism within African American communities and provides an introduction into the three major black Methodist denominations.

Sernett, Milton C. *Bound for the Promised Land: African American Religion and the Great Migration.* Durham, N.C.: Duke University Press, 1997. Sernett's book represents one of the few studies of religious developments in African American communities (and by extension the entire nation) as African Americans moved in large numbers into cities during the Great Migration of the late nineteenth century and early twentieth century.

Washington, James Melvin. *Frustrated Fellowship: The Black Baptist Quest for Social Power.* Macon, Ga.: Mercer University Press, 1986. This book remains one of the few studies devoted to the black Baptist churches from the mid-eighteenth century to the formation of the National Conventions. Readers will appreciate the way in which Washington links the development of religious institutions to the formation of sociopolitical and economic identity.

Weisenfeld, Judith, and Richard Newman, eds. *This Far by Faith: Readings in African-American Women's Religious Biography.* New York: Routledge, 1996. Readers interested in additional information on the role of women in the development of black religious identity and institutions should give attention to the biographical pieces presented in this book.

Wilmore, Gayraud S. *Black Religion and Black Radicalism: An Interpretation of the Religious History of Afro-American People,* 2nd ed. Maryknoll, N.Y.: Orbis Books, 1983. Wilmore's book provides a framework for understanding the impact of African American religion on all recent scholarship in black religious studies. He argues that black religion is shaped by an often troubled relationship with progressivism and provides examples of earlier progressive leadership in black churches and concludes with examples of similar activity as expressed through black liberation theological thought. He also notes that for much of the late nineteenth century through the 1940s, black churches are deradicalized—that is to say, they are more strongly marked by a quest for spiritual renewal than social transformation.

PART ONE

The Development of the Black Church

CHAPTER 1

African American Methodist Churches

The Development of Methodism

John Wesley, the founder of Methodism, was born in 1703 in Epworth, England, into a family well acquainted with the workings of the Anglican Church. Strongly influenced by a popular doctrine calling for the strictly monitored use of time, Wesley applied this approach to his religious life by devoting more attention to refining the inner life as a way of monitoring external events and appetites. He extended this disciplined Christian life to include work on behalf of others (such as missions), which resulted in John and his brother, Charles, accepting an invitation to travel to the North American colony of Georgia. The trip did not include Christianizing Indians, enslaved Africans, and others but did entail a rethinking of the evidence of salvation. Upon returning to England this questioning, combined with the advice of some who claimed salvation by faith alone, resulted in Wesley's conversion experience in 1738. As many scholars have noted, this conversion did not result in a drastic change in theological outlook. Instead he developed a renewed interest in evangelism through traveling ministry. Preaching in a variety of venues marked the remainder of Wesley's life.

Unlike some on the evangelist trail, Wesley was concerned with more than the soul's condition. He recognized that converts needed organizational structures and networks that allowed continued growth and fellowship. Because the zeal and interest generated by a sermon quickly faded, something was needed to rekindle the religious fire that led to salvation and Christian conduct. During his early years as a traveling minister, Wesley worked out a system of societies and ritual materials intended to buttress the Anglican Church.[1] Activities included *love feast* services and *watch-night* services. A love feast was a gathering in which members of the society were free to speak about their religious struggles and victories. A watch-night took place periodically on a given Friday and involved a meeting with prayer, singing, and preaching that began late in the evening and continued until shortly after midnight. Although materials such as the Anglican Church's *Book of Common Prayer* were used, the style of worship and the emotional energy that characterized Methodist society worship were foreign to most Anglicans. The emotional nature of these meetings, as well as its theological emphasis on conversion and relationship with God, mark the evangelical thrust of the societies.

Methodist societies, so called because of their fixed structure and systematic approach to the Christian life, did not base membership on strict regulations and doctrinal commitments. Those seeking fellowship needed only to present themselves as sincere seekers of righteousness, saved by faith alone, with the ability to answer properly questions related to their salvation. This conversion experience, as Hester Ann Roe's account attests, was a wrenching and angst-filled process entailing a faith-based acceptance of God's grace that was a clear move away from Calvinist notions of predestination:

> [H]er life had been unsatisfactory in that she had experienced no personal relationship to God. . . . Again, stealing away to hear Samuel Bardsley, the Methodist, preach, she was deeply moved: "I thought every word was for me. He spoke to my heart as if he had known all the secret workings there; and pointed all such sinners, as I felt myself to be, to Jesus crucified. I was much comforted." Again the respite was short and incomplete. . . . At last she comes to her crisis. She had been reading a pamphlet given to her by Cousin Charles Roe: "The Great Duty of Believing on the Son of God." "I was much encouraged in reading this, and would gladly have spent the night in prayer. . . . I prayed but it seemed in vain. I walked to and fro, groaning for mercy; then fell again on my knees; but the heavens appeared as brass, and hope seemed almost sunk into despair; when suddenly the Lord spake that promise to my heart, 'Believe on the Lord Jesus Christ, and thou

shalt be saved.' I revived, and cried, 'Lord, I know this is Thy word, and I can depend on it. But what is faith?' . . . Again it came, 'Only believe.' 'Lord Jesus,' said I, 'I will, I do believe: I now venture my whole salvation upon Thee as God; I put my guilty soul into Thy hands, Thy blood is sufficient. I cast my soul upon Thee for time and eternity.'"[2]

Centralization of the societies was important to the success of Methodism. The activities of each society were centralized to monitor growth and to address problems. Regional meetings took place throughout the calendar year that brought individual societies together. In addition, Wesley began calling a larger meeting—the conference—which brought together traveling ministers from various regional meetings to report on their spiritual and financial efforts. The conference, first held in 1784, became the governing body of the Methodist societies. Even with this structure in place, Wesley maintained control over the societies until his death.

One can imagine that friction existed between Methodist societies and the Anglican Church. This was the case for several reasons: (1) the organizational structure of the Methodist societies (for example, traveling ministers appointed by Wesley) did not fit with the hierarchy of the Anglican Church; (2) the style of worship and the more loosely defined requirements for membership and ministry made the society fellowship attractive and resulted in a decline in attendance at Anglican church services; and (3) although orthodox, the theological leaning of the Methodists challenged the doctrinal and ritual framework of the Anglican Church through, for example, a more frequent celebration of communion.

In spite of growing tension, John Wesley wanted to maintain links with the Anglican Church. Yet the break in 1791 was inevitable. Wesley provided the final impetus by appointing three superintendents responsible for the growing Methodist societies in North America (1784). In so doing, he assumed the authority held by Anglican bishops to appoint and ordain ministers. From Wesley's perspective these appointments were necessary to continue the effective work being done by Methodist evangelists who could not administer important rituals such as baptism without the presence of a superintendent. In the newly independent United States, the Anglican Church no longer filled this function, but Wesley would not allow the potential for saving souls to be lost.[3]

Methodism in the United States

Some scholars argue that Philip Embury was the first to give a Methodist sermon in North America and that he was followed in 1769 by two itinerant ministers, Joseph Pilmoor and Richard Boardman. Others note that Charles Delamotte remained in Georgia for six months after Wesley's departure in 1738, in order to provide guidance for the small group of North American Methodists, and Delamotte was followed by evangelist George Whitfield.[4] Although these evangelists and others like them were important, it is the work of Francis Asbury, sent in 1771, that provided a major North American Methodist thrust. Asbury was resolved to spread the gospel even during the early years of his time in the United States. The growth of Methodism in America is due in large part to the zeal of ministers, exemplified and inspired by Asbury, who traveled trade routes to the Southeast, Northwest, and West, and who battled theological opposition from those in New England. Traveling preachers used the circuit system to spread Methodism:

> The circuit system meant that a preacher served not one community, but a whole group of communities. These circuits varied in size. In the newer countries, where settlements were much scattered and far between, they covered many square miles of territory, and the preacher occupied from four to six weeks in making the rounds of the circuit. Nor was he particular where he conducted his services; a log cabin, or the barroom of a tavern, or out under the trees. . . . He preached whenever and wherever he found anyone to listen, with little regard to either time or place. . . . A young man who showed any ability in public speaking was urged by the class leader and the circuit preacher to exercise his gift on every possible occasion, and when the presiding elder came around . . . the young man was recommended for an exhorter's or local preacher's license. He did not often travel a circuit, but he preached in his own and neighboring communities and in many instances was instrumental in organizing new classes in frontier settlements before the regular circuit rider or presiding elder arrived upon the scene.[5]

Under the leadership of Asbury, the Methodist Episcopal Church was formed in the United States in 1784, years before the emergence of an independent Methodist Church in England. The success of Methodism was met often with objections and condemnations for a number of reasons, including: (1) Methodist worship offended those who maintained the supremacy of high worship; and (2) the code of conduct embraced by Methodist ministers and congregations was contrary to the southern socialization process and code of honor. Those who objected to Methodism sought to disrupt services in a variety of ways: "The most common form that opposition took between 1770 and 1810 was for critics to interrupt Methodist worship services. No setting was off-limits, whether the services were in private homes, groves, courthouses, or church buildings. . . . The intent of many who interrupted services was ostensibly just to disrupt those present. These scenes, however, follow the contours of shaming rituals, with their ultimate object being the collective dishonor of Methodists. One man loudly cracked nuts throughout a service; another came in the middle of a sermon smoking a cigar."[6] Such efforts failed to dissuade Methodist congregations. If anything, it steadied their resolve to seek out the lost and bring them into the Christian family.

African Americans and Methodism

In addition to their concern for the welfare of white Americans, Methodists showed a strong interest in "saving" Africans.[7] According to an entry in Asbury's diary:

> It is of great consequence to us to have proper access to the masters and slaves. I had a case, a family I visited more than a year ago, a tyrannical old Welshman. I saw there he was cruel, his people were wicked, and treated like dogs. "Well," say you, "I would not go near such a man's house." That would be just as the devil would have it. In one year I saw that man much softened, his people admitted into the house of prayer, the whole plantation, 40 or 50 singing and praising God. What now can sweeten the bitter cup like religion? The slaves soon see the preachers are their friends, and soften their owners towards them. There are thousands here of slaves who if we could come out to them would embrace religion. It is of vast moment for us to send the news far and wide. It hath its influence.[8]

Although the vast majority of Africans at this time remained unfamiliar with the Christian gospel, the Methodist Church's growth is undeniable. For example, as of 1791, there were roughly 11,680 African Methodists and their numbers increased until they accounted for almost one-fourth of the total church membership by 1797. By 1861, the Methodist Church contained roughly 210,000 Africans.[9] Much of this growth stemmed from camp meetings that were

> generally held in the summer time—in some central position, on an elevated spot, shaded with beautiful oak and hickory trees, and where water can easily be obtained. The camp consists of a circle of tents, numbering from fifty to three hundred, made of plank or canvas. The space included within the first circle of tents, excepting the avenue for walking or promenading, is consecrated to religious worship. Within this inclosure a rough and substantial pulpit is erected, immediately in front of which is a place denominated the altar, where those who seek the forgiveness of their sins come forward to be prayed for. Still further on are seats for the white congregation. *Behind the pulpit, and separated by a board fence, is the place allotted for the colored people.* . . . But by no class is a camp-meeting hailed with more unmixed delight than by the poor slaves. It comes at a season of the year when they most need rest. It gives them all the advantages of an ordinary holiday, without its accompaniments of drunkenness and profanity. (Italics added)[10]

According to many sources, Africans preferred separate services because they could worship away from the watchful eyes of slaveholders. "Slaves assembled separately at the camp meetings, as one white observer explained, so they could enjoy the 'freedom in speaking, singing, shouting, and praying they could not enjoy in the presence of their masters.' This freedom of expression was circumscribed, however, by the attendance of some whites at slave church services to ensure that nothing occurred which could be construed as subversive of the system."[11] Even when segregation—forced or volunteer—took place, it is possible that the Methodist approach to salvation, through a marked and often traumatic conversion experience, served as an equalizer because the rich and free had no greater access to heaven than the poor and enslaved. In this way, converts, having accepted God's gift of eternal life, belonged to a community that corrected for some shortcomings and uncertainties of an unjust society. Methodism, as expressed during the revivals and camp meetings, could be used by both free and enslaved Africans to make sense of the world and help create a more humane way of life.

Some scholars argue that enslaved Africans found Methodist (and Baptist, as we shall see) services appealing because of the importance placed on the sacrament of baptism, which reminded Africans of water rituals and cults that many practiced in Africa. Likewise, the importance of the felt presence of the Holy Spirit in Methodist services through shouting and possession harkened back to a similar importance placed on spirit possession in West African religious practices. In this way, Methodism provided an intellectual and ritual link between the two worlds known by enslaved Africans. Furthermore, the emphasis on spiritual deliverance, as illustrated by Old Testament stories, was appealing and beneficial because of the implications for physical freedom. Some Methodist ministers, including Africans who had greater access to pulpits in Methodist meetings, made an effort in their sermons to speak to the sufferings endured by Africans.[12]

> The initial discipline of the denomination, in keeping with the thought of Wesley, denounced the slave system because it was contrary to the golden law of God, on which hang all the laws and the prophets, and the unalienable rights of mankind, as well as every principle of the Revolution, to hold in the deepest debasement, in a more abject slavery than is perhaps to be found in any part of the world except America, so many souls that are capable of the image of God. We therefore think it our most bounden duty to take immediately some effective method to extirpate this abomination from among us. . . .[13]

Beyond openly criticizing the slave system, Asbury believed the work of Methodists should destroy the system of slavery by restricting membership to those who did not hold slaves. Perceived as threatening to the economic welfare of planters, these efforts by Methodist ministers were met with wide resistance. Assumed connections between Methodist teachings and slave revolts fueled this resistance. In order to maintain access to the mission field, many within the Methodist Episcopal Church made peace with the slave system because, in the long run, "the mission of the Church was to 'preach the Gospel to every creature,' Negro as well as white. If indignant masters kept them from the slaves, the preachers reasoned, negroes would never know of God's love for them. And the master, alienated by harsh rules, would shut himself away, not only from his own salvation, but also from influences that would work ultimately to free the slaves."[14] Thus, the notion of common redemption or spiritual freedom for all did not mean freedom on earth. Methodist preachers reconciled their concern for enslaved Africans with the demands of slaveholders by emphasizing the saving of the soul irrespective of the physical body's fate. The issue of slavery ultimately resulted in a split within the Methodist Church along regional lines, the anti-slavery North and the pro-slavery South.

◆

In summary, John Wesley, the father of Methodism, committed his life to disciplined Christian work. In his itinerant ministry, he used the Anglican Church's *Book of Common Prayer*. However, the nature of the Methodist worship style and its emphasis on conversion and one's relationship with God was not understood or accepted by the Anglican Church. To supplement the worship experience provided by the Anglican Church, John Wesley formed Methodist societies. In 1791, when John Wesley appointed three superintendents for the growing Methodist societies, he was accused of usurping the power of the Anglican bishops. Wesley's efforts within the societies ultimately resulted in a break with the Anglican Church. Even prior to this break, Methodists made their presence felt in North America through the effort of hard-working preachers, such as Francis Asbury. Under Asbury's zealous leadership the Methodist Episcopal Church was founded in the United States in 1784. Methodism was successful in America in part because its ministers were willing to go "into the highways and byways" to preach the gospel. The Great Awakenings associated with the 1700s and the 1800s matched the emotional and energetic worship associated with Methodism. The Great Awakenings brought the Gospel of Christ to both whites and blacks. Francis Asbury and others argued that the gospel was meant for all humans, regardless of color. This perspective was enforced through the denial of membership to whites who were slaveholders. The issue of slavery would ultimately split the Methodist Church into a northern branch and a southern branch, but by this time blacks had already embraced the Methodist Church and were working to make it their own.

Study Questions

1. What caused the final split between the Methodist Societies and the Anglican Church?
2. What are three of Methodism's defining features?
3. How did Methodism spread in North America?

4. Why did enslaved Africans find Methodism attractive?
5. What was responsible for the success of Methodism during the Great Awakenings?

The African Methodist Episcopal Church

The development of the African Methodist Episcopal Church draws together both the experiences of freedom and of slavery, which is demonstrated by the life of the founder of the denomination, Richard Allen. Before his removal to Dover, Delaware, Richard Allen and his family were the slaves of Benjamin Chew, a lawyer in Philadelphia. Under the influence of Methodist preaching, Allen was converted in 1777 and encouraged to enter the ministry. His preaching eventually bore fruit when the conversion of his owner resulted in an opportunity for Allen to purchase his freedom by working for hire off the plantation. Shortly after he secured his freedom, Francis Asbury and other Methodist ministers gave Allen preaching opportunities, including one at St. George's Methodist Episcopal Church in Philadelphia, the church where Asbury first preached in North America.

Richard Allen
(Courtesy of University of North Carolina Library at Chapel Hill)

Although Allen only intended to stay in Philadelphia a short time, he became established there as a highly respected and successful member of the community. In 1787, Allen and several others developed the Free African Society as a mutual aid society to address the full range of needs of African Americans that were not addressed in the regular church gatherings and social opportunities of Philadelphia. This benevolent organization helped provide moral guidance and financial assistance as part of living a Christian life.

It became clear that this mutual aid society had to take on additional responsibility for the welfare of its members. The rapid growth in the numbers of African worshipers at St. George's propelled discussion of issues charged with implicit racism, such as where should Africans sit and how should they participate in services? In 1787, when African members were physically prevented from praying at the altar, they withdrew from the church vowing never to return. Allen described the incident in this way:

> A number of us usually sat on seats placed around the wall, and on Sabbath morning we went to church, and the sexton stood at the door and told us to go in the gallery. He told us to go and we would see where to sit. We expected to take the seats over the ones we formerly occupied below, not knowing any better. We took those seats. Meeting had begun, and they were nearly done singing, and just as we got to the seats the elder said, 'Let us pray.' We had not been long upon our knees before I heard considerable scuffling and loud talking. I raised my head up and saw one of the trustees. . . . Having hold of the Rev. Absalom Jones, pulling him off his knees, and saying, 'You must get up; you must not kneel here.' Mr. Jones replied, 'Wait until prayer is over.'. . . . He came and went to William White to pull him up. By this time prayer was over, and we all went out of the church in a body. . . .[15]

At this point, what had started as a society to supplement the inadequate assistance received from whites became an African church. White Methodist leaders were unhappy with this development, and they made their feelings known. Debate with St. George's continued until 1816 when legal action (the Methodist Episcopal Church sued when a white elder was denied the new church's pulpit) worked in the new church's favor, freeing it from the control of ministers appointed by St. George's Methodist Episcopal Church. With this decision, the African church was able to completely break ties with the Methodist Episcopal Church. Most of the society members who formed the African church held an interest in joining the Church of England. But Allen convinced them that "plain doctrine and . . . good discipline" were important and were best attainable through Methodism. "Beholden to the Methodists," he and a few others purchased an old blacksmith shop and, moving it to Sixth near Lombard, turned it into a place of worship. It was dedicated by Francis Asbury as Bethel Church in 1794, and Allen was ordained by Asbury in 1799.[16]

The church continued to grow and received word from other areas of the country (such as New Jersey and Maryland) where African Methodists experienced similar hardships and sought ways of freeing themselves from religious and social constraints. These common issues and worries resulted in these various congregations uniting under the banner of the African Methodist Episcopal Church in Philadelphia on April 9, 1816. With one thousand people, they formed the first African American denomination in the United States based on this resolution: "Resolved, That the people of Philadelphia, Baltimore, and all other places, who should unite with them, shall become one body under the name and style of the African Methodist Episcopal Church [AME Church]."[17]

At the first conference in 1816, they began the task of uniting these various societies with rules and regulations, since a common name, AME, was not enough. Because leaving the Methodist Episcopal Church was not based on a doctrinal disagreement, they chose to use the Methodist Episcopal Church's *Book of Discipline*, but strengthened its anti-slavery stance. The new denomination also recognized the need for a leader who would guide the new church. Daniel Coker was elected the first bishop; however, he was more interested in missionary activity in West Africa. Therefore, Richard Allen was elected in his place, and he served in this capacity while pastoring Bethel Church in Philadelphia. The needs of the church eventually dictated the selection of additional bishops to monitor church life throughout the network of churches. Bishops were chosen to be responsible for particular regions of the church, and a general council of bishops was developed as a way to provide supervision for the church as a whole. With respect to codes of ethical conduct, the AME denomination embraced the general rules of the society established by Wesley—calling for proper dealings in business and other relationships, temperance, respect for scripture, and mild conversation. Punctuality, proper dress, and cleanliness for members were also considered vital. The church believed the ramifications of proper conduct and appearance were far reaching because Africans might receive better social, economic, and political treatment if they presented themselves properly. To carry out this agenda, organizations such as the Benevolent and Temperance societies were developed.

AME Church Timeline

1787	Free African Society formed
1787	Africans removed from prayer at St. George's AME Church
1794	Bethel Church dedicated by Francis Asbury
1799	Richard Allen ordained Free African Society formed
1816	African Methodist Episcopal Church formed as first African American denomination
1816	Richard Allen elected first bishop of the new denomination
1827	AME foreign missions underway in Canada and Haiti
1856	Wilberforce University founded
1863	Henry McNeal Turner becomes first African American chaplain
1864	AME and AME Zion churches consider merger
1864	AME Church begins work with former slaves in the South
1884	*AME Church Review* founded
1885	Benjamin W. Arnett elected to Ohio legislature as first African American to hold this office from a majority white area
1895	Henry McNeal Turner proclaims "God is a Negro"
1896	The Women's Home and Foreign Missionary Society formed
1900	Reverdy C. Ransom organizes the first Institutional Church and Social Settlement House within the denomination
1936	Martha J. Keys, a Kentucky pastor, introduced a bill at the General Conference in New York to ordain women
1944	Women's Missionary Society formed
1948	Rebecca M. Glover ordained
1954	Brown (Oliver Brown) vs. Board of Education
1956	Department of Worship and Evangelism formed
1960	General Conference authorizes the ordination of women as itinerant deacons and elders
1960s	James H. Cone pioneered the development of Black Theology
1964	Carrier Hooper first woman to run for the bishopric
1965	Mother Bethel designated a National Shrine by the Department of the Interior

During each of the first four years of the denomination's existence, meetings called annual conferences were held in both Philadelphia and Baltimore. The officials present remained a relatively small group, yet the general membership of the denomination continued to grow, reaching eight thousand by 1839.[18] The growth of this new denomination was not solely dependent upon absorbing existing congregations that were discontent with their denominational affiliations. Like Methodist circuit riders before them, AME ministers conducted revival services and camp meetings, increasing the fold through the converting of souls. Additionally, the fledgling denomination made provisions for spreading the word to those beyond their borders by distributing printed materials from its publication department. The Book Concern Department (today known as the Sunday School Union) developed in 1818 and was the first publishing house in the United States created and owned by African Americans. With time AME publications would include journals such as the *African Methodist Episcopal Church Review* (1884) and newsletters that provided information regarding particular church issues and more general topics such as abolition.

Implicit in the development of these written materials was a concern with literacy and education, and no one did more to increase the educational emphasis of the AME Church than Daniel Alexander Payne. Born to free parents in Charleston, South Carolina, Payne opened a school in Charleston, but hostility from some whites resulted in the passing of laws prohibiting education for Africans. Payne closed the school and left the South but did not give up his interest in education. His efforts eventually resulted in the founding of the AME Church's Wilberforce University in Ohio (1856). For many whites this focus on education, combined with claims of independence, marked the AME Church as a dangerous organization. In addition, slave rebellions, such as the one in which AME minister Morris Brown was implicated, closed most plantations to evangelists, particularly evangelists from the North whose very presence could spark ideas of freedom. Until the Civil War, which brought relative security through the presence of federal troops, AME ministers were more active outside the Deep South. When they did receive access to southern areas before the Civil War, restrictions limited their effect, such as in New Orleans where they could speak only to free Africans and only before sunset. Even if they were allowed to preach to slaves in places like Washington, D.C., creativity and ingenuity were essential because direct comment on physical freedom would end access (and possibly life).[19]

The task of domestic missions was always consistently embraced, but what was always less certain was the role of women in the church vision of ministry. From the church's early years, leaders—including Richard Allen—did not see the necessity of including women in ordained ministry, preferring to encourage their involvement as informal prayer band leaders, deaconesses, stewardesses, and so on, who worked under the authority of men. This was certainly the case with Jarena Lee who, feeling called to preach, approached Richard Allen only to be told there was no precedent in the *Book of Discipline* for the ordination of women: "I now told him [Allen], that the Lord had revealed it to me, that I must preach the gospel. He replied by asking in what sphere I wished to move? I said, among the Methodists. . . . He said that our Discipline knew nothing at all about it—that it did not call for women preachers."[20] After much consideration, Lee found this response troubling and out of line with the biblically chronicled workings of God. She responded:

> O how careful ought we to be, lest through our by-laws of church government and discipline, we bring into disrepute even the word of life [Bible]. For as unseemly as it may appear now-a-days for a woman to preach, it should be remembered that nothing is impossible with God. And why should it be thought impossible, heterodox, or improper, for a woman to preach? Seeing the Saviour died for the woman as well as the man. . . . Did not Mary first preach the risen Savior, and is not the doctrine of the resurrection the very climax of Christianity—hangs not all our hope on this, as argued by St. Paul? Then did not Mary, a woman, preach the gospel? For she preached the resurrection of the crucified Son of God.[21]

Although never ordained, Lee and others like her sought opportunities to preach as exhorters. Some of the church's male leadership began to recognize the unacceptable nature of this restriction on ministry. In 1888, Henry McNeal Turner ordained a woman only to have the ordination ruled invalid by the general conference. It was not until 1948 that a woman, Rebecca Glover, would be ordained and have that decision approved by the conference.

The experience of forerunners to Glover such as Lee points out the manner in which the AME Church, in its effort to achieve mainstream status and respectability in the eyes of the larger society, embraced social sensibilities and attitudes that restricted the participation of the majority of its members, namely, black women. The participation of women in aspects of ordained ministry has increased over the years, culminating in the ordination of a woman to the office of bishop. However, most women involved in AME Church ministry continue to face discrimination and limitations on their activities. But even when not involved in ordained or formal ministry, women have always worked to secure the money and other resources necessary for the church to undertake mission activities.

Concerning domestic missions, it was not long after the Emancipation Proclamation that AME ministers and missionaries made their way south to spread the gospel and minister to the physical needs of the former slaves. In 1865, two years after the church sent James Lynch and J. D. S. Hall to South Carolina, Payne traveled south and organized a conference that included North Carolina, Georgia, and South Carolina (for which the conference was named). Four thousand new members entered the church through this conference. The work of Lynch and Hall sparked efforts that would eventually include some seventy missionaries sent south by 1870. By the time of the second annual meeting of the South Carolina Conference, the church's membership was close to fifty thousand; and by 1876 it claimed approximately three hundred thousand members. Before the twentieth century, the denomination contained more than twenty-two conferences spread across North America, with a combined membership of over two million.[22]

Development of the AME Church in the South was not strictly the result of AME efforts to advance the Kingdom of God on earth. In addition, many white congregations encouraged African members to leave and join churches "better suited" to them. Despite this push, for many former slaves, joining the AME Church was an opportunity to exercise freedom and liberty long denied. Free persons make decisions and dictate their own direction; they do not have to submit to monitored worship services or biracial services if they do not find such worship acceptable. Typically, many freed men and women took their invisible religious institutions (discussed in the introduction) and placed over them a visible framework in the form of the AME Church.

The work of the church with respect to missions demonstrates the manner in which its perspective was in keeping with a sense of chosenness. That is to say, the AME Church understood itself as elected by God to bring salvation and to uplift the unfortunate members of its race. The Civil War and Reconstruction were, for AME missionaries, a sign of God's displeasure with the system of slavery as well as God's call for the evangelizing of the elusive South. Yet the job was difficult because of limited excess to transportation and harassment from those who did not want southern society changed by northern sensibilities.

Even when missionaries did not encounter open hostility, it was not uncommon for them to lack accommodations and for their fledgling churches to be without a house of worship. In these cases preaching the gospel had to be combined with a business sense and construction skills. Nonetheless, by the end of the Civil War and Reconstruction (1876), the AME Church was firmly established in the South and the Midwest. Through the efforts of Henry McNeal Turner and his contemporaries, the AME Church remained on the cutting edge of political issues and maintained a focus on the general health and welfare of African Americans. Unmatched as a church leader in the nineteenth century, Turner developed within the AME Church a brand of nationalism that pushed the limits in order to achieve recognition of the physical importance of blackness through statements such as "God is a Negro" (1895) and by denouncing American racism. In addition, Turner was one of the AME Church's strongest supporters of emigration, arguing that it was part of God's plan for African Americans:

> There is no more doubt in my mind that we have ultimately to return to Africa than there is of the existence of a God; and the sooner we begin to recognize that fact and prepare for it, the better it will be for us as a people. We there have a country unsurpassed in productive and mineral resources, and we have some two hundred millions of our kindred there in moral and spiritual blindess. . . . And as soon as we are educated sufficiently to assume control of our vast ancestral domain, we will hear the voice of a mysterious Providence, saying, "Return to the land of your fathers."[23]

According to Turner, the AME Church had an obligation to fulfill this call and to take the gospel to Africa. Missionary activity allowed the AME Church to respond to missionary zeal in a way that countered the racism of organizations such as the American Colonization Society that sought to rid the United States of its free African American population under the guise of missions. Work in Africa grew and in the late 1800s AME conferences were created in Sierra Leone in West Africa, and Pretoria, Queenstown, Orange River, and Cape Town in South Africa. Before World War I, the AME Church claimed missionary workers in eight countries, two bishops on foreign soil, and in Africa alone it had more than one hundred ordained ministers and four times as many unordained ministers with better than seventeen thousand members.

The twentieth century marked new socioeconomic and political crises. Rather than the question of slavery, the church was faced with a disenfranchised community that had moved recently in large numbers into cities as part of the Great Migration, which was due to poor agricultural opportunities in the rural South and the promise of industrial employment in urban areas. Because of the development of mass inner city life and the changing nature of the African American community, the AME Church had difficulty responding to and speaking for the African American community at large. An exception to this policy was Reverdy C. Ransom, who was born in Flushing, Ohio. He urged the denomination to live out the social ramifications of the Gospel of Christ, in keeping with its own rhetoric. Through this approach, Ransom and others like him responded in meaningful ways to the misery experienced by African Americans. Like Richard Allen before him, Ransom undertook this theological and religious task by speaking to the value of African American humanity and by relating this to the love of God in ways that fostered self respect, self determination, and improved standing in both this world and the next. Any attempt to work on behalf of God had to be expressed, according to Ransom, through attempts to better the human family.

Over the course of time, the AME Church's infrastructure has changed to accommodate its agenda, sense of mission, and the needs of more than two million members. As of the mid-twentieth century, one could expect local churches to have at least five levels of leadership (including minister, trustees, stewards, stewardesses, and deaconesses). In addition, there were typically at least as many auxiliaries and departments (including the Sunday school, missionary department, evangelism, usher board, and young people's department). On the national level, the goals and objectives expressed on the local level were also expressed through offices and departments. For example, by the mid-twentieth century the church included the various conferences (general, annual, and district) responsible for monitoring the operative dimensions of the church as well as bishops, presiding elders, itinerant ministers, and nonordained ministers and laity. In addition, it contained numerous departments such as Christian education, missions, pension, publications, social action, and so on, that allow for both national and international operations.

◆

In summary, Richard Allen, the founder of the AME Church, was converted after hearing a sermon by a Methodist preacher. Encouraged to enter ministry, it became evident that Allen had an understanding of God's concern with the needs of blacks. In Philadelphia, he became involved with St. George's Methodist Episcopal Church and played a role in the formation of the Free African Society (1787). Racist practices at St. George's ultimately resulted in the members of the Free African Society leaving the church and forming Bethel Church, under the leadership of Richard Allen. This place of worship was dedicated by Francis Asbury, who also ordained Allen. The members of Bethel Church realized that they were not alone; other African churches had formed as a result of racial discrimination. In 1816 several of these churches met with Bethel Church and formed the African Methodist Episcopal Church, the first African American denomination developed in the United States. With time, this denomination grew to include a publication department and other auxiliaries geared toward helping to spread the message of Christ to African Americans throughout the country. Although the church's primary concern remained the United States, AME missionaries were also sent to Africa and the Caribbean before the start of the twentieth century. While quick to recognize the needs of African Americans with respect to both religious and secular issues, the AME Church was far slower to include women within the church's hierarchy. In fact, it was not until 1948 that an AME woman was ordained.

Selected Leaders of the AME Church

MORRIS BROWN (1770–1849). Born in Charleston, South Carolina, Brown eventually joined the AME Church and was ordained in 1817. He served numerous congregations and often used his church as a place to help and hide fugitive slaves. A member of his church, Denmark Vesey, led an unsuccessful insurrection in 1822 to which Brown was assumed an accomplice. This made life dangerous for Brown and he left for Philadelphia where he joined Bethel Church and was consecrated the second bishop within the denomination in 1828. Brown's hard work for the church was remembered and celebrated in part through the naming of a college after him, Morris Brown College of Atlanta, Georgia.

MARY G. EVANS (1891–1966). Evans was born in Washington, D.C., but spent her early years traveling as the adopted child of an itinerant minister. Feeling called to preach at an early age, Evans's abilities were recognized and she was licensed to preach as a teenager. She spent much of her time developing her abilities and the educational background she felt incumbent upon would-be ministers. In 1924, Evans became the first woman to receive the Doctor of Divinity degree from Wilberforce University. Word of her preaching abilities continued to grow and she gained a reputation as one of the most powerful evangelists in the denomination. During the 1920s she became one of the first women to pastor a church within the denomination.

JARENA LEE (1783– date unknown). Lee was born in New Jersey and experienced a strong need for conversion that resulted in sickness and emotional pain. Moving to Philadelphia some time after her twenty-first birthday, Lee encountered the preaching of Richard Allen and was converted shortly thereafter. Some time later, after questioning her faith, Lee was sanctified and called to preach. She expressed this calling to Richard Allen who acknowledged her preaching abilities but refused to ordain her. Instead Lee was granted permission to work as an exhorter and, according to some accounts, was the first woman licensed to preach by the new denomination. She spent much of her time holding very successful services as an evangelist.

REVERDY C. RANSOM (1861–1959). Ransom was born in Ohio to a mother who showed great concern for his education and who worked to ensure his eventual success. In 1882 Ransom began his studies at Wilberforce University and experienced his conversion during his first year. After this experience Ransom joined the AME Church, and upon graduation he pastored a string of AME churches, rising through the ranks. His commitment to the physical and spiritual welfare of African Americans took full form during his pastorate in Chicago when, in 1900, he developed the Institutional Church and

Social Settlement House. This was the first major social gospel thrust in the AME Church. Although the model was rejected by many within the denomination, Ransom continued to gain stature within the church. He eventually served in key positions such as editor of the *AME Church Review* and eventually as one of the church's bishops. In addition to his church work, Ransom was known for his socialism and his interaction with key racial uplift figures, such as W. E. B. DuBois.

HENRY McNEAL TURNER (1834–1915). Turner is rightfully recognized as one of the most radical churchmen of the late nineteenth and early twentieth centuries. Born in South Carolina, Turner was free but well aware of the horrific institution of slavery. Self-educated for the most part, Turner valued knowledge and applied it in a variety of ways. In 1851 he joined the Methodist Episcopal Church and began his travels as a preacher. Seven years after joining this denomination, Turner encountered the AME Church and found its independence and pro-Black stance appealing. He joined and began to move through its ministerial ranks. The Civil War, the failure of Reconstruction, and his encounter with Alexander Crummell troubled Turner and resulted in a growing separatist inclination. Contrary to the dominant opinion within the church, Turner became an outspoken advocate of the Back-to-Africa movement. This, however, did not damage his continuing development within the church, marked by his becoming a bishop in 1880. His positions were often controversial and a prime example of this is his attempt to ordain women long before the 1948 ordination of Rebecca Glover.

Study Questions

1. What factors brought about the formation of the AME Church?
2. How did the AME Church undertake missions in America?
3. How and when did the AME Church begin its foreign missions program?
4. How would you explain the role of women historically in the AME Church?
5. How did the AME Church connect its social mission with the Gospel of Christ?

Suggested Reading

Andrews, William L., ed. *Sisters of the Spirit: Three Black Women's Autobiographies of the Nineteenth Century.* Bloomington: Indiana University Press, 1986. This text provides first-hand reflections on the dilemma faced by black women during the nineteenth century who expressed an interest in ministry. The pieces provide reflections on their conversions, call to preach, and perspective on ministry. It provides much needed attention to the role of black women in the development of the church, and it fills in some of the holes in the above presentation.

Campbell, James T. *Songs of Zion: The African Methodist Episcopal Church in the United States and South Africa.* New York: Oxford University Press, 1995. This is one of the few comparative treatments of the AME Church. Readers interested in the nature of both domestic and foreign missions within the AME Church will find this book useful.

Gregg, Howard D. *History of the African Methodist Episcopal Church: The Black Church in Action.* Nashville: AMEC Sunday School Union, 1980. Gregg's book provides interesting information on the development of the AME Church in a manner sensitive to both insider and outsider concerns.

Payne, Daniel A. *History of the African Methodist Episcopal Church.* New York: Arno Press and the New York Times, 1969. Readers interested in the early history of the AME Church from the perspective of its leadership will find this book helpful. Payne, one of the church's early leaders, provides a discussion that is sensitive to issues of education for clergy and other themes important during the church's formative years.

Walker, Clarence E. *A Rock in a Weary Land: The African Methodist Episcopal Church during the Civil War and Reconstruction.* Baton Rouge: Louisiana State University Press, 1982. This book gives readers insight into the motivation for and method used in the AME Church's domestic mission efforts during a major period of growth.

The official website of the AME Church is www.amecnet.org. This site contains information on the church's history, current projects, and leadership.

The African Methodist Episcopal Zion Church

The African Methodist Episcopal Zion Church (abbreviated AME Zion, also AMEZ) has its roots at John Street Church in New York. As the size of the congregation at John Street Church increased, proper accommodations for white members made the presence of Africans problematic. Both St. George's Church, discussed earlier, and John Street Church decided on the same solution: segregated seating and restricted access to important rites and rituals (with Africans praying while whites took communion). In response, Peter Williams and others representing the African membership petitioned Francis Asbury for permission to hold regular meetings of their own beginning in 1796, "in the intervals of the regular preaching hours of the white church," and in this way they could freely "invite their coloured brethren yet out of the ark of safety to come in."[24] The request was approved and four years later, Zion Church was built and incorporated as the African Methodist Episcopal Church of the City of New York.

When another church developed, with former Zion member William Miller preaching, the circuit was expanded to include both Zion and the new congregation called Asbury Church. Although controlled by their African membership, these churches remained under the jurisdiction of the Methodist Episcopal Church, led by a John Street Church elder. In 1820, William Stillwell, the white elder responsible for Asbury and Zion churches, left his role because of what he considered unfair financial arrangements between the dominant Methodist Church of New York, John Street, and other churches. Asbury and Zion churches were without leadership. Their request for a new conference and the ordination of African ministers met with mixed response. News of the plight of the Zion and Asbury churches brought word of similar concerns elsewhere. In response, interested churches from New York, Connecticut, and Pennsylvania—representing over 1,410 African American Methodists—met in 1821 in New York and formed a new conference under the continued jurisdiction of the Methodist Episcopal Church. This meeting was followed by a second gathering one year later attended by nineteen delegates representing churches in New York and Philadelphia.[25]

In spite of an appeal to Methodist Episcopal Church bishops, the new conference received no assistance. Arrangements were made to have William Stillwell and two other white ministers ordain James

Varick, Abraham Thompson, and Leven Smith as elders in 1822. Even after this was done, Varick and the others hoped to remain within the jurisdiction of the Methodist Episcopal Church. Yet from the perspective of the Methodist Episcopal Church, African Methodists had severed their relationship through the development of their own book of discipline, *The Doctrines and Disciplines of the African Methodist Episcopal [Zion] Church in America* in 1820, as well as the selection of its own elders. In 1824, the General Conference of the Methodist Episcopal Church made it clear that it would not support African Methodists who formed their own book of discipline and ordained their own ministers. African Methodists viewed this response as an attack on their religious equality. In response, the various churches met and formed the African Methodist Episcopal Church in America (some sources say "in New York"); the addition of "Zion" occurred in 1848, to distinguish this group from the African Methodist Episcopal Church, which had formed earlier. Like the AME Church, the name of the denomination was explained in its catechism as representing the historical heritage of the members in Africa and the doctrinal connection to John Wesley's Methodism. Although the denomination's name gives special attention to the African heritage of its founders, the church has always been open to all and concerned with the welfare of all.

Zion Church and the other churches within the new denomination could have joined forces with the AME denomination, but earlier experiences with Allen counseled against such a link. As recorded by historian Carol V. R. George, Allen agreed to ordain William Lambert a minister for the Zionites in New York. However, upon his return to New York, Lambert established a new church rather than ministering at Zion Church. It seemed obvious to Zion's membership that Allen was responsible for this and was using it as an opportunity to establish the AME Church in New York.[26]

Although not affiliated with the AME Church, the Zion denomination held similar interests expressed through the vision of laypersons and clerical leaders. Early leaders included James Varick, who became the church's first district superintendent (or bishop). Under the preaching influence of Philip Embury, Varick, at age sixteen, came into contact with the evangelical teachings of the Methodist Church. After his conversion, he joined John Street Church and was licensed to preach.[27]

AME Zion Church Timeline

1796   Request made to hold separate meetings

1800   African American Methodists from St. John's build a church

1801   Church incorporated as the African Methodist Episcopal
Church of the City of New York

1820   New church built

1821   New conference of Black Methodists founded

1821   James Varick elected bishop

1822   James Varick ordained

1829   Foreign missions developed in Canada

1848   New denomination adds Zion to its name

1864   Missionaries sent South

1876   Missions started in Africa

1880   Livingstone College founded

1880   Ladies Home and Foreign Mission Convention founded

1890   *The AME Zion Quarterly Review* founded

1894   First woman ordained, Julia Foote

1898   First woman ordained as elder, Mary Jane Small

1909   Young Woman's Society formed

1924   Bishop assigned to Africa

1928   AME Zion Church develops ten mission stations in Ghana,
serviced by native missionaries

1934   Barber Memorial Camp founded in West Granville,
Massachusetts

1944   Brotherhood Pension Service established

1946   Sesquicentennial of the denomination

1952   James C. Hoggard Sr. named first corresponding
secretary to visit all Zion foreign missionary fields

1953   Harriet Tubman's home, owned by the church, rebuilt

1958   Board of foreign missions incorporated in Washington, D. C.

1962   Devotional booklet "The Strength of My Life" introduced to
the church by Raymond L. Jones

1962   New building for the Cartwright Memorial Church (Mother
Church of Africa) built in Brewerville, Liberia

1966   Stephen G. Spottswood placed on the Executive
Committee of the 11th World Methodist Conference

1966   Emma B. Watson, of the Woman's Home and Foreign
Missionary Board, named representative to the World
Federation of Methodist Women

1967   Herbert Bell Shaw elected chairman of the Board of
Directors for the National Conference of Black Churchmen

The work begun by leaders such as Peter Williams and James Varick was continued through luminaries such as Christopher Rush of North Carolina. Rush knew first-hand the plight of those seeking escape from bondage. In fact, at age twenty-one, he reached New York City, having escaped slavery. After his arrival, he became a Methodist and joined Zion Church shortly after its formation. Feeling a call to preach, he was licensed in 1815 and ordained in 1822. Throughout his long career, Rush worked toward preparing African Americans for full citizenship and all its benefits through the Phoenix Society and the American and Foreign Antislavery Society as well as the Convention of the Colored People of the United States. According to some, Rush was the primary architect of this denomination's activities and under his leadership the church increased from two thousand members in 1831 to almost five thousand in 1840.[28]

The Civil War provided access to the southern states in ways that promoted tremendous growth, much of which took place through the leadership of Superintendent J. J. Clinton and the effort of laypersons such as Eliza Ann Gardner. Before his work as a superintendent, Clinton labored in various areas including Canada. He was initially reluctant to accept responsibility for the conference that included many of the southern states because there were limited resources for sending missionaries. But in 1864 Clinton sent five missionaries—James W. Hood, Wilbur G. Strong, John Williams, David Hill, and William F. Butler—to North Carolina, Florida, and Kentucky, among other areas. Although the missionaries met with some success, the work of Hood stands out. In North Carolina, Hood brought churches in Beaufort, New Bern, Wilmington, and Fayetteville into the denomination. He also played a role in the development of Fayetteville State University. Due to Hood's work, Clinton could call the North Carolina Conference for its first meeting in 1864, with four hundred members and twelve ministers. By 1900, the denomination claimed roughly a half million members in over thirty-six hundred churches, served by roughly twenty-five hundred ministers. By the mid-twentieth century it claimed a membership of almost one million.

AME Zion missionaries entered the field with enthusiasm but encountered the same difficulties experienced by AME missionaries: poor transportation, limited funds (and church property), and hostile residents who were reluctant to tolerate any display of African American independence. Nonetheless, the work resulted in more than thirty conferences spread across the country before the turn of the century. In addition to missions in the U.S., which were a priority, the AME Zion Church, like the AME Church, worked in foreign fields as well. Work in Canada began in 1829 through a petition made by a church located in Prescott, Upper Canada. The AME Zion Church also made inroads into Africa through Andrew Cartwright, the first Zion missionary in Africa, who sailed for Liberia in 1876. Within four years, Cartwright had established three churches. As was the case with the AME Church, missions efforts were not the sole domain of men, and women such as Harriet Mae Green, a registered nurse, missionary Arwilda G. Robinson, missionary Lillian Tshabalala, and others played a major role. Although this work had its high and low points, by 1932, the Zion denomination counted about eighteen thousand members in West Africa. Early missionaries in the Caribbean included J. W. Lacey who made his way to Haiti in 1861, but his stay was short and his efforts short-lived. He returned to the United States in 1869 and never returned to mission work. Beyond these failed attempts, the church was able to do more substantive work in Jamaica, British Guiana (changed to Guyana), Demerara (South America) and the Virgin Islands. By 1877 there was a conference organized in the Bahamas and in 1948 a conference for the Virgin Islands was established.

Some of this missionary work, both domestic and foreign, was no doubt aided by the church's growing number of publications. In 1876 the church began publishing the *Star of Zion*. In addition, Zion established the *AME Zion Quarterly Review* in 1890. Like the *AME Review*, this quarterly sought to provide compelling discussions of pressing issues and concerns. Creation of these reading materials attested to an education platform that included the development of schools such as Livingstone College (1880) as well as Booker T. Washington's Tuskegee Institute, which started in the basement of Butler Chapel, an AME Zion Church in Tuskegee, Alabama. Much of the work culminating in the development of various institutions of higher learning began with the Sunday School Union (1872). Its work was ultimately placed under the jurisdiction of the education department (1892, later becoming the Christian Education Department in 1924). In addition to the Christian education department, the early Christian Endeavor Society (through the Varick Christian Endeavor Society) was embraced by Zion churches to bring Christian morals and knowledge to young people.

Beyond developing the mechanisms necessary for creating printed materials and educational opportunities, it should come as no surprise that church growth required a more complex organizational structure. As of 1872, the church already consisted of bishops, ministers (both ordained and lay), presiding elders, and departments such as the Women's Home and Foreign Missionary Society. Over the course of time, the church developed new departments and boards such as Christian education, evangelism, finance, home missions, foreign missions, publication house, and so on, in order to maintain the progress of the denomination and its missions.

James W. Hood
(CourtesyUniversity of North Carolina Library at Chapel Hill)

The AME Zion Church's success was probably enhanced through its recognition of the role women could easily play in spreading the gospel. With respect to women in ordained ministry, it must be noted that the AME Zion Church opened its doors to women long before the AME Church. In fact, Hood began ordaining women in 1894 with Julia Foote. Foote, who converted at the age of fifteen, believed like Jarena Lee in the full process of sanctification. In her autobiography she outlines the process of her conversion and sanctification which culminated in a call to ministry: "nearly two months from the time I first saw the angel, I said that I would do anything or go anywhere for God, if it were made plain to me. He took me at my word, and sent the angel again with this message: 'You have I chosen to go in my name and warn the people of their sins.' I bowed my head and said, 'I will go, Lord.'"[29] Foote "went forth laboring for God, and he owned and blessed my labors, and has done so wherever I have been until this day.

And while I walk obediently, I know he will, though hell may rage and vent its spite."[30] Even with the ordination of Foote and other women, the vast majority of the women involved in the AME Zion Church, as was the case in the AME Church, worked through departments and programs designed for their input, such as the Female Benevolent Society. Although the participation of women in the various levels of ordained ministry has increased over the years, there continues to be few women at the highest levels of authority.

Like the AME Church, the AME Zion denomination grew during the period of the Great Migration, but this also marked a period of turmoil and a general rethinking of the church's responsibilities and goals. In the words of one of its ministers, Calvin Marshall III:

> There is no doubt in my mind that the Zion Church from its beginning, up through the abolitionist movement, the Civil War, and Reconstruction, clearly saw itself as a church whose mission was one of liberation. One only has to read the life stories of some of her leaders and follow the minutes of many of her annual and general conferences to realize that the undergirding motivation of this organization was the acquisition of full freedom for the black man in America. Unfortunately, as the church entered the twentieth century other things and other priorities seemed to replace the burning zeal that the church once displayed for liberation.[31]

African Americans were lured to northern cities by the promise of a better life based upon industrial jobs. Progress, however, was illusionary but the needs of these migrants were real, and the church felt taxed in trying to meet these needs. As AME Zion bishops noted, "in view of the fact that a large majority of those who migrated will remain permanently in the North, East and Northwest, notice is served upon us to help provide for them or else we will have labored short of the demand, and others will have entered into our labor."[32] The AME Zion denomination did not escape the introspection and reevaluation of goals and attitudes that other African American denominations confronted during the twentieth century. On the contrary, it confronted these issues on a variety of levels as it attempted to maintain its reputation as the "freedom church." To do so, it needed to develop ways to act out its social gospel.

The social agenda of the church often remained inactive during the early twentieth century. Even so, figures such as George L. Blackwell sought new methods of addressing the problems associated with the Great Migration. In 1919 the Tercentenary Drive was developed under his leadership with a two-fold purpose: to remember the arrival of Africans to North America three hundred years before and to secure funds, one million dollars as the goal, by which to affect the life options and welfare of African Americans. The drive fell below the goal, and attention was turned to maintaining if not increasing the denomination's membership and property holdings. The church did not surrender its progressive mission but, in fact, sought to more fully participate in the social issues of the day. For example, involvement in organizations such as the National Fraternal Council of Churches (1934), designed to unify African American Christian efforts to impact issues of social justice, and participation in the Civil Rights movement, serve as examples of this commitment.[33]

◆

In summary, the AME Zion Church developed when black members of John Street Church in New York faced discrimination similar to that faced by black Methodists at St. George's Church in Philadelphia. With the permission of John Street Church and Francis Asbury, Peter Williams and others formed the African Methodist Episcopal Church of New York City. With time this church, called the Zion Church, was followed by the formation of Asbury Church. When the white elder responsible for the leadership of these two churches left, they petitioned for the formation of a conference within the Methodist Episcopal Church. In 1821 this conference was formed and elders were ordained, but the General Conference of the Methodist Episcopal Church opposed it as a threat to the authority of the Methodist Church over its members. Trouble between this new conference and the General Conference resulted in the formation of the African Methodist Episcopal Zion Church as a separate denomination. Like the AME Church, this new denomination worked, through figures such as James Hood, to ensure the religious and material success of African Americans in both the North and the South. With growth in membership, the denomination developed new programs, departments, and auxiliaries to spread its teachings and perspective on social issues in the United States and foreign fields such as Africa and Canada. Much of the success of the AME Zion Church resulted from the efforts of black women who received ordination as early as 1894 and who also worked through departments such as the Women's Home and Foreign Missionary Society.

Selected Leaders of the AME Zion Church

JOSEPH JACKSON CLINTON (1823–81). Born in Philadelphia, Clinton is recognized as a central figure in the church's early expansion during the Civil War and Reconstruction. First converted in 1838, Clinton was ordained in 1840 and started his career as a church builder. His activities resulted in his election as the youngest bishop (at age thirty-two) in the church's history. As the first bishop responsible for the church's southern region, Clinton organized over a dozen conferences and increased the number of ministers serving the region. Under Clinton's leadership, James Walker Hood conducted his historic work in North Carolina.

FLORENCE SPEARING RANDOLPH (1866–1951). Unlike many women in the church with a call to preach, Randolph exercised this vocation as the pastor of several churches. Born in South Carolina, Randolph moved north and became a member of Monmouth Street AME Zion Church in New Jersey. Under the supervision of an AME Zion minister, Randolph began studying scripture and began preaching during holiness meetings and other services. Her success as an exhorter earned her recognition as a local preacher, and in 1901, after a long struggle, she was ordained a deacon (and an elder two years later). Her abilities in the pulpit gained her the pastorate of several churches, but once they became viable congregations she was always moved to make room for a male minister. In addition to pastorates, Randolph held other positions such as founder of the New Jersey Federation of Colored Women's Clubs.

MARY JANE SMALL (1850–date unkown). Small, who was born in Tennessee, became the first woman ordained an elder in the church. After holding various positions in the church, Small had a conversion experience at the age of twenty-three, and in 1890 she voiced a call to preach. For two years she suppressed this calling until the burden became too much and she sought recognition of this vocation. She was licensed to preach and ordained a deacon in 1895. In addition to other work, Small was president of the Woman's Home and Foreign Missionary Society.

JAMES VARICK (1750-1827). Varick was born in Orange County, New York, and played a major role in the development of the AME Zion Church. Having joined John Street Methodist Church in 1766, Varick became one of the first deacons ordained in the new denomination. His work on behalf of the new church proved invaluable and he was consecrated the church's first bishop. He is commonly referred to as the church's founder. Varick's activities included the development of the church's book of regulations. He also played a major role in abolition activities outside the church through his work with *Freedom's Journal*, the first African American newspaper in the country.

ALEXANDER WALTERS (1858–1917). Walters was born into slavery. Through the churches of Kentucky, he was exposed to educational opportunities. This connection to the church continued from his initial membership in 1870 through his eventual elevation to the position of bishop. Walters was licensed to preach in 1877 and ordained in 1879. This official sanction was followed by pastorates of various churches. His success in the pastorate resulted in his selection as the head of the church's Book Concern in 1889. At age 33, he was elected a bishop of the church. From this position he worked for the uplift of African Americans through involvement with the Niagara movement (forerunner of the National Association for the Advancement of Colored People) and the National Colored Democratic League, which played a major role in the election of Woodrow Wilson to the presidency. In addition to domestic advancement, Walters also pushed the United States to give attention to Africa. As part of this project, he encouraged African Americans to migrate to Liberia.

Study Questions

1. What caused the split within John Street Church?
2. How did the AME Zion Church undertake missions in America?
3. How and when did the AME Zion Church begin its foreign missions program?
4. How would you explain the role of women in the workings of the AME Zion Church?
5. What were the mechanisms used in outreach activities of the church?

Suggested Reading

Davenport, William H. *Membership in Zion Methodism: The Meaning of Membership in the AMEZ Church.* Charlotte, N.C.: AMEZ Publishing House, 1936. This is an early study of the AME Zion Church's sociopolitical and religious motivation and aims, and the impact of these factors on church membership. A basic question answered is: What attracts African Americans to this denomination?

Baptiste, Louis. *Basic Beliefs of the African Methodist Episcopal Zion Church.* Charlotte, N.C.: AMEZ Church School Editorial Section, 1964. The title of this book says it all. Baptiste presents the basic theology and doctrine embraced by the church.

Townsend Gilkes, Cheryl. *If It Wasn't for the Women: Black Women's Experience and Womanist Culture in Church and Community.* Maryknoll, N.Y.: Orbis, 2000. This is a unique study drawing on some of Townsend-Gilkes's earlier work on the forms of power exercised by women within the Black Church. It is an important supplement to the above history (and chapters 2 and 3 as well) of the Black Church's activities and growth.

Walls, William J. *The African Methodist Episcopal Zion Church: Reality of the Black Church.* Charlotte, N.C.: AME Zion Publishing House, 1974. This is one of the few available histories of the AME Zion Church. It provides important information on its development (dates, names, places, and so on) not presented above.

AME Zion Church's official website is www.theamezionchurch.org.

The Christian Methodist Episcopal Church

With the end of slavery the Methodist Episcopal Church, South, realized missionaries from the North would ultimately take many of its members. This fear was justified because more than half the Africans involved in the Methodist Episcopal Church, South, left during the Civil War and Reconstruction period. It was clear that a separate body for Africans was necessary and desirable, if the Methodist Episcopal Church, South, wanted to keep an African presence. Thus, the Christian Methodist Episcopal Church developed not out of protest over racial discrimination within the church setting and was not solely the product of Africans establishing their own religious institutions as a form of protest. On the contrary, there was cooperation between the Methodist Episcopal Church, South, and its African members.

At a meeting held in 1870 at Liberty Church in Jackson, Tennessee, Southern Methodists worked out the plans for this new church, the Colored Methodist Episcopal Church (CME). The church was named based on the following premise: "Whereas we are a part of that same Church [Methodist Episcopal], never having seceded or separated from the Church, but in the division of the Church by the General Conference in 1844 we naturally belonged to the South, and have been in that division ever since; and now, as we belong to the colored race, we simply prefix the word 'colored' to the name, and for ourselves adopted the name, as we are in fact a part of the original Church, as old as any in America; therefore be it Resolved, I. That our name be the 'Colored Methodist Episcopal Church in America.'"[34]

This name was later changed to the Christian Methodist Episcopal Church in 1956. The CME Church is similar to the AME and AME Zion denominations in that it too embraced the *Book of Discipline* used by the larger body of Methodists, with only minor changes in order to make it "conform . . . to our name and the peculiarities of our condition."[35]

A leadership plan was put into place, beginning with the election of two bishops, William H. Miles and Richard H. Vanderhorst. Miles had been a member of the Zion denomination for a short period of time, and Vanderhorst had once belonged to the AME Church. Both were former slaves. The general makeup of the denomination, with respect to departments and committees, resembles the AME and AME Zion churches. That is to say, like the others, the CME Church maintains its internal and external commitments through a series of auxiliaries, departments, and officers responsible for overseeing the church's work. In addition to having the same hierarchy of bishops, presiding elders, ordained ministers, and non-ordained ministers, the denomination also had, by the mid-twentieth century, more than ten departments including missions, evangelism, Christian education, and publications.

William H. Miles
(Courtesy of University of North Carolina Library at Chapel Hill)

The new denomination's connection to the Methodist Episcopal Church, South, had some benefits—particularly concerning finances—but this connection was often used against the church during its mission efforts in the South. Both AME and AME Zion missionaries, for example, remarked that the CME Church was the church of those who had favored slavery and joining it would not be an exercise of freedom and liberty. When this tactic did not work, AME and AME Zion ministers often attempted to take over CME Church (as well as Methodist Episcopal Church) property. But even with these annoyances, the CME Church began operating without some of the hardships faced by both the AME and AME Zion churches because, at its moment of inception, it already had forty thousand members. As of 1873, three years after its founding, the denomination claimed a membership of over sixty-seven thousand divided into fourteen annual conferences. Less than fifty years later, it would have more than seven hundred thousand members.

Although developed for different reasons, the CME Church shared the same interests and concerns as the AME and AME Zion denominations. In all cases there was a concern with providing educational opportunities for freed men and women. The CME Church's first successful effort resulted in the establishment of Lane College, begun in 1882 as Jackson High School. Early leaders of the denomination considered the establishment of educational institutions a necessary component of its major mission to bring the Gospel of Christ to the masses. In the words of one of the early bishops, Lucius Holsey:

"[The Church's] aim is evangelization of the colored race. First, by preaching the pure and simple gospel of Christ to the masses, in the simplest form of speech. Second, to do this in the best and most effective manner, we aim, as far as possible, to establish and maintain schools for the impartation of Christian education among our people, and especially among the ministry, and that part of the race who are expected to be teachers."[36] Other attempts to influence the life options of African Americans required additional infrastructure for the church, such as the departments of finance, missions, Christian education, evangelism and Woman's Missionary Society as well as publications such as *The Christian Index* (1867).

CME Church Timeline

1859 William H. Miles ordained a deacon in the Methodist Episcopal Church, South

1870 Colored Methodist Episcopal Church formed

1870 William Miles and Richard V. Vanderhorst elected bishops

1882 Establishment of Jackson High School, which later became Lane College

1917 Women's Connectional Missionary Society (Women's Missionary Council) formed

1917 Mattie Elizabeth Coleman elected first president of the Missionary Society

1918 Women's Missionary Council recognized by the General Conference

1947 Missions in Ghana begin

1954 Church begins ordination of women

1956 Church name changed to the Christian Methodist Episcopal Church

1960s Church begins full-scale foreign missions

1963 Henry C. Burton led CME members in the March on Washington

1970 National Headquarters established in Memphis, Tennessee

With respect to women in ministry, the CME Church is similar to the AME Church in that both denied women ordination until the twentieth century. The CME Church ordained its first women pastors in 1954. However, two of the women who exercised their ministries in the CME Church prior to this date are Quinceila Whitlow and

F. E. Redwine. Having begun decades after both the AME and AME Zion churches, and having begun mission work outside the South late, the CME Church did not develop organizations through which women participated in the growth of the church, such as the Home Missionary Society and the women's Connectional Missionary Council, until the first decade of the twentieth century. Although its platform on domestic missions and developments was in place long before this period, it was not until the 1960s that the CME denomination undertook substantial work in Africa. This move into foreign missions was the result of an invitation from Joseph Wright to take control of a school he ran in Ghana. Before this, the church did some missionary work in Zaire with the assistance of the Methodist Episcopal Church. The church's work in Nigeria and South Africa emerged in 1960.

The CME Church concentrated on the United States for most of its history and, unlike both the AME and AME Zion denominations, it avoided in most cases, involvement in Reconstruction politics as well as hot button issues such as emigration or the Back-to-Africa movement. This is not surprising considering its positive relationship with the Methodist Episcopal Church. Its early leaders thought that cooperation with whites was the key to racial harmony, and in keeping with this agenda the Methodist Episcopal Church, South, was thought of as providing "fatherly directorship."[37] Isaac Lane acknowledges that it might be difficult for some to understand the mutually beneficial relationship between the CME Church and Methodist Episcopal Church, a relationship he described as "a fraternal sympathy, a mutual good will, a kindly interest that made the relation cordial and highly helpful."[38] A notable exception to this apolitical stance is the work of Lucius Holsey, the youngest person ever consecrated a bishop in the CME Church. Along with Henry McNeal Turner of the AME Church, he was a major advocate of African American separatism. Yet Holsey's stance was not as militant and his rhetoric not as biting as Turner's. When speaking of the claim of African Americans to the United States and their relationship to Africa he wrote: "We regard him as a part of the people, a permanent fixture in the United States of America. It is true, we hope, that many of the race will, some day, go to Africa—their native land—but the masses will fight the battle of life here, and live and die on the American continent. We also recognize the fact that he is, and will be, singularly and collectively, a separate and distinct race from the others."[39]

Despite his insistence that the CME Church was not a "little slave church" beholding to white Methodists, Holsey was often criticized for not getting involved in Reconstruction politics, to which he replied that ministers of the gospel could not behave and operate in the same way as politicians. Leaders such as Holsey argued that the Christian gospel, when preached properly, fitted the converted with a moral code that could transform the world. The church's mission is to provide this moral base, not to become involved in the political process. By making this statement, Holsey is not suggesting African Americans should avoid political involvement such as exercising the right to vote. The right to vote was purchased with much blood shed by many African Americans. Rather, he is suggesting that, unlike the AME and AME Zion preachers, CME ministers should provide the gospel from the pulpit and stay away from political platforms. In his words: "While our ministry and members represent all political parties and creeds, yet, as ministers of the gospel, we make no stump-speeches and fight no battles of the politicians. We think it better to 'let the dead bury the dead,' while we follow Christ. Of course we have no control over any man's vote; whether he be minister or member, he is free to vote as he pleases. We regard Christianity not only as reformatory and redeeming, but as a moral power of civilization."[40]

In more recent years, the CME Church has taken a more overtly political stance against social injustice. The denomination's position on various issues is more radical and it is more politically involved in the life of African American communities, especially with its attack on racism. This is done without surrendering the centrality of the Christian vision of the church and its initial commitment to unity and cooperation between the races.

◆

In summary, with the end of slavery, the Methodist Episcopal Church, South, realized that northern African American churches would recruit in the South and take away many of its members. To maintain some of its black membership, a meeting was held in 1870 during which the Colored Methodist Episcopal Church was formed, which later changed its name to the Christian Methodist Episcopal Church in 1956. Although the CME Church differed from the other black denominations on political issues in that it refused to become involved in Reconstruction's political and social dimensions, it shared their concern for evangelizing recently freed slaves. CME Church members believed that political issues should be addressed from the political stage, and the church's pulpit should be reserved for preaching the gospel. Before the twentieth century, the church concentrated on establishing new churches and developing institutions of higher learning in the United States. During the mid-twentieth century, the CME Church began foreign missions in Africa, and it also finally allowed women access to a full range of church ministries through ordination.

Selected Leaders of the CME Church

Helena Brown Cobb (1870–1915). Before becoming a public school principal and teacher, Cobb received a B.A. degree from Atlanta University in her home state of Georgia. Her relationship with the CME Church began with her marriage, in 1899, to a minister. As a minister's wife, much of Cobb's energy went into the development of structures for women's involvement in missionary activities. Along this line, in 1902, she was elected president of the Georgia Conference Mission Society. In addition, in 1906 she became the first editor-in-chief of the *Missionary Age* magazine. Maintaining her interest in education, Cobb founded in 1908 the Helena B. Cobb Industrial Institute for Girls, which was the only school within the CME Church for women. Her interest in a denominational missionary organization did not bear fruit until after her death.

Caesar David Coleman (1919–). Coleman, born in Mississippi, was the son of a CME minister. Knowing he would follow his father into ministry, by 1950 Coleman received his B.A., M.A., and B.D. Two years later, he began work as a pastor and college professor. Quickly moving through the ranks, he became a presiding elder in 1956. Through his election to the church's Board of Christian Education, Coleman played a major role in the development of the Interdenominational Theological Center in Atlanta (1960), which is the largest African American center for theological studies in the world. He became a bishop of the church in 1974 and continued his work through organizations such as the National Congress of Black Churches.

Mattie Elizabeth Coleman (1879–1942). Born in Tennessee to parents affiliated with the AME Church, Coleman changed her membership when she married a CME minister in 1902. In 1906, she completed medical training at Meharry Medical College and began her practice in Tennessee. Much of her work was with the poor, and she combined medical services with religious attention to human needs as president of the District Missionary Society. It was under her leadership and in response to her work that the General Conference undertook the formation of the Women's Missionary Council. Coleman combined her leadership of the Council with leadership as dean of women at Lane College.

Joseph Carlyle Coles Jr. (1926–). Coles was born and educated in Washington, D.C. After his ordination, Coles pastored a variety of churches. In Ohio, where he distinguished himself through his work with the denomination's Ohio Leadership Training School and as a member of the Cleveland Board of Education. After years in the pastorate, Coles was elected a bishop in 1974. His stature extends beyond the CME Church in that he also served on the World Methodist Council's executive board. He is known for his work during the Civil Rights movement.

Lucius Henry Holsey (1842–1920). Holsey was born a slave in Georgia. Although he lived for some time with a family on the University of Georgia campus, he received no formal education. After the emancipation of the slaves, Holsey continued his interest in religion, which first developed as a child. In 1868 he was licensed to preach by the Methodist Episcopal Church, South, and was sent to Savannah to begin his ministry. He was part of the conference in which the CME Church was formed, and in 1871 Holsey became pastor of one of the new denomination's major churches. Two years later he was elected the church's youngest bishop ever. His commitment to education was well known, and he played a major role in the development of the church's publishing house, as well as being instrumental in the founding of Paine College and Lane College.

Study Questions

1. What motivated the formation of the CME Church?
2. What was the relationship between the CME Church and the Methodist Episcopal Church, South?
3. What was the initial mission of the CME Church?
4. How did this initial mission change over time?
5. What has been the role of women in the church's work?

Suggested Reading

Lakey, Othal Hawthorne. *The Rise of "Colored Methodism": A Study of the Background and the Beginnings of the Christian Methodist Episcopal Church.* Dallas: Crescendo, 1972. As the title suggests, this book provides a basic history of the CME Church. It provides details and a perspective that nicely supplements the rather brief presentation above.

Montgomery, William E. *Under Their Own Vine and Fig Tree: The African American Church in the South, 1865–1900.* Baton Rouge: Louisiana State University Press, 1993. This book is not limited to the CME Church. It provides a history of black churches that brings into context the major black churches during the period of the Civil War through the early phases of the Great Migration.

Phillips, Charles Henry. *The History of the Colored Methodist Episcopal Church in America.* New York: Arno Press, 1972. This book provides a basic and interesting history of the CME Church.

Sernett, Milton, ed. *Afro-American Religious History: A Documentary Witness,* Durham: Duke University Press, 1985. This is a collection of speeches and sermons by prominent figures within the Black Church. It is not limited to the CME Church, but it does help to bring the issues of concern to this denomination into context.

The website for the CME Church is www.c-m-e.org.

CHAPTER 2

African American Baptist Churches

The Development of the Baptist Faith

The story of the Baptist faith in America begins with John Smyth. Smyth was a Separatist (that is, a person who desired separation from the Church of England on religious grounds) preacher in Gainsborough, England, who moved with his group to Holland, due to persecution. Smyth and the members of his church argued that baptism should *only* take place when an adult—any adult—has repented and made a confession of faith in Jesus Christ. Based on this doctrine, Smyth rebaptized himself and the members of his congregation in an effort to move closer to an understanding of the church as God would have it. What resulted from this act was the development of the first Baptist church in Holland. In Smyth's words: "wee professe even so much as they object: That wee are inconstant in erroer: that wee wou'd have the truth, though in many particulars wee are ignorant of it: We will never be satisfied in indevoring to reduce the worship and the ministry of the Church, to the primitive Apostolic institution from which as yet it is so farr distant."[1]

This search for a purer fellowship with God and fellow Christians was not without conflict. For example, those Smyth followers who began questioning his interest in and eventual merger with the Mennonites left and developed a Baptist church outside London under the leadership of Thomas Helwys. Helwys had been a part of Smyth's group and retained the understanding of salvation as open to all who confess a belief in Jesus Christ (1612).[2] In spite of persecution, Baptist churches in England grew and developed a general assembly in 1671.

In addition to this doctrine of general salvation, there were Baptist churches in England that held to a Calvinist understanding of salvation for only an elect few.[3] These Baptists were called Particular Baptists because of their belief in redemption for only a select or particular group of humans. Other Baptists were labeled General Baptists because of their belief in salvation as available to all. There were strong differences between these two groups of Baptists, but there was also a common push to transform the church. Both communions believed in the reformation of the official church by moving away from the compromise and corruption they saw in the Church of England (and the Roman Catholic Church). In this sense both sought a separation from communities and doctrines that prevented a full life in keeping with biblical principles and the workings of the original church discussed in the New Testament. Some groups distanced themselves from the Church of England and its corrupt political powers, but Baptist congregations went much further by seeking a complete separation (hence the name *Separatists*), which is reflected in its doctrines of no ordination by Church of England bishops and no infant baptism as promoted by the Church of England. With regard to the latter point, it was reasoned based on scripture (John 3:5) that infants were too young to make a confession of faith and act upon it. Hence, only adults could fulfill the requirements of baptism. Simply put, baptism was only for believers, and only believers were the true members of the church. In the North American colonies, a similar perspective was present in the teachings of figures such as Roger Williams.

The Baptist Church in America

In England, Roger Williams served as Sir William Masham's chaplain. This position freed Williams from some of the constraints associated with a church appointment and allowed him to maintain his rather Separatist perspective regarding the Church of England's structure and worship. From his perspective, the formulaic nature of church worship prevented a deep spiritual connection with God. Proper church structure was necessary if fellowship with God was to be fully realized. For Williams and others, this entailed a *covenanted congregation* with membership strictly limited to those who are "professing and practicing Christians" and who publicly rejected association with the troubled Church of England. Only those who met these requirements were in a proper spiritual position for correct worship and holiness.[4] Separatists like Williams believed the Church of England made a mistake in thinking Christendom could be defined geographically, when Christendom was rightfully defined as the community of all who confess Jesus Christ and work toward holiness. Although Williams was initially content to maintain his Separatist beliefs in England, he eventually left for New England. Williams made his home in Massachusetts, but his firm commitment to rejecting publicly the Church of England as a prerequisite for membership in the true community of believers posed a problem. Williams demanded a complete separation with the Church of England, while many people living in the Massachusetts Bay Colony believed it was possible to live a righteous life without a complete rejection of the Church of England. Williams and his wife left Boston for Salem but officials in Boston prevented him from becoming a teacher in the Salem church. In response, Williams made his way to Plymouth where he stayed for two years (1631–33) before returning to Salem. Beginning in 1633, Williams argued for a more radical separation from the Church of England than most were comfortable with. In short, Williams's call for separation from the Church of England could mean rejection of family, friends, and civil authority (when necessary) because the regenerated should have *no* fellowship with the unrepentant. Furthermore, he believed true Christians were in a position to interpret scripture for themselves, under the guidance of the Spirit of God, and, furthermore, to prophesy.[5] Williams's group was a minority, but the energy with which Williams asserted their beliefs caused problems. Ultimately, Williams was expelled from Massachusetts because of his views. Leaving Massachusetts in 1636, Williams and his followers formed a community along the Great Salt River, which Williams called Providence. Each member of this community was granted a plot of land, and each agreed to be governed by a set of communally developed rules and regulations. In 1644 Williams received permission from the English Parliament to unite Providence with Portsmouth and Newport under the name Providence Plantations, within the colony of Rhode Island.[6]

Basic tenets in this new commonwealth were religious freedom and the separation of church and state. The latter, separation of church and state, stems from Williams's argument that the church lost its authority during the Middle Ages and that Christians during the seventeenth century represented a "new" Israel guided by the gospel. Furthermore, he argued, the government had no authority with which to control this new Israel. In other words, the Old Testament contained a depiction of Old Israel, but "after the coming of Christ. . . . Old Israel was no longer a model for church *and* state, but only for the church."[7] Williams's group survived and, based on its doctrine of religious liberty, became home to numerous religious communities. Although Williams's commitment to the Baptist perspective would be short-lived, it is in this colony that the first Baptist church in North America was developed in 1639.

In Rhode Island, as in Europe, division developed between those who believed the death and resurrection of Christ served to redeem an "elect" group—the John Calvin-influenced Particular Baptists—and General Baptists who argued for Christ's gift of redemption for all humanity. With time, associations (that is, groups of congregations based on region) of Baptist congregations began developing in New Jersey and Pennsylvania as well as states further south. The Particular Baptist perspective was dominant during this early phase but this did not prevent other perspectives. The autonomy of Baptists and the thrust for religious growth during the mid-eighteenth century fueled two major groupings of Baptist: New Light or Separate Baptists and Old Light or Regular Baptists. The development of these communions is complex and beyond the scope of this book. However, in short, while both groups were "poor and disinherited," the Separate Baptists were revival-minded and enthusiastic in worship while the latter were not.[8]

The eastern portion of North America, from Rhode Island to Georgia, was exposed to the Baptist faith through the work of Baptist evangelists as well as the religious fervor of the period. In southern areas, congregations developed as a result of Separate Baptist revival fervor, complete with energetic singing and celebration of God's goodness during worship. This expression of religious commitment came with equally energetic demands for proper daily conduct. Failure to fulfill expectations with regard to Christian living could result in expulsion from the religious community. Historian Mechal Sobel describes a typical week for those who embraced Separate Baptist faith: "Sundays were fully the Lord's day, with meetings held morning and afternoon. Midweek prayer meetings, monthly business meetings, and special extended prayer meetings, or revivals, structured the social life of members. All other forms of social life were suspect, if not actually proscribed. Itinerary was an important institution. Preachers traveled widely, stopping at Baptist homes. . . . occasionally, whole congregations moved together to bring the word to new areas."[9] Baptist churches appealed to many, including enslaved Africans who were often treated as religious equals, including all the accompanying opportunities and responsibilities. Put another way, "The relatively disinherited, looking for a faith that would indeed give promise that they, too, might share equally in all of God's gifts, found fulfillment in this Baptist faith and polity. The church was the community of believers. Once accepted, a man was the equal of everyone else in the church."[10]

African Americans and the Baptist Church

Many enslaved Africans who were permitted by their owners to attend revival services and camp meetings embraced the Baptist faith. In addition to the strong appeal of emotional elements of worship, Baptists showed limited concern for educational qualifications for preaching and with memorizing catechisms. No doubt that Africans found the preaching of these Baptist evangelists appealing because it often condemned institutions that prevented humans from fulfilling God's will, such as the slave system. In opposition to ungodly systems of oppression, Baptists preached the equality of all believers and the autonomy of local communities of the faithful. In this sense, for poor whites and enslaved Africans, the Baptist message promised full humanity and democracy despite the restrictions of the unchurched world.[11]

By the 1800s much of the theological friction between Separate and Regular Baptists had eased. Through this blending Baptist churches became more acceptable in the South, but acceptability required a less consistent denunciation of the slave system. Successful evangelists had to be sensitive to the concerns of slaveholders. When slaveholders believed conversion posed no threat, they supported it; however, when it was perceived as a danger to the slave system, slaveholders prevented religious instruction. In either case, social inequality took preference over religiosity. James Smith, a former Virginia and Georgia slave, points to this white suspicion in a 1852 interview, which is recounted by Henry Bib:

> [James Smith] became a convert to the Christian religion, and made application to the Baptist Church one Sabbath-day to be admitted into the church and the ordinances of baptism: but the minister refused to have anything to do with him until he could see Brother Wright (his master), who was a member of the same church, about it. After the preacher had seen his master, who consented that he should be baptized if he should be found worthy after being examined. . . . On the day appointed, he was accordingly examined: many questions were asked him, to which he answered and gave general satisfaction, but before he was discharged, his master had one or two questions to ask, namely: "Do you feel as if you loved your master better than you ever did before, as if you could do more work and do it better?" "Do you feel willing to bear correction when it is given you, like a good and faithful servant. . . ."[12]

In spite of white resistance and suspicion, Africans were converted. The first African Baptist on a church roll was at a church in Newton, Rhode Island, and by the early 1770s the Baptist church in Boston began to reflect African membership in its records. Africans in northern churches, however, remained second-class members with virtually no opportunity for leadership and a limited voice with respect to the workings of the church.

The religious situation for Africans was in many respects far worse in the South. Nonetheless, the first African Baptist churches were southern churches—the congregation on William Byrd's plantation in Mecklenburg, Virginia (1758) and the Silver Bluff Church (of Silver Bluff, South Carolina). The latter was founded by George Liele and managed by one of his converts. Liele had a conversion experience after hearing a Baptist preacher, Matthew Moore, give a sermon:

> [H]e unfolded all my dark views, opened my best behavior and good works to me, which I thought I was to be saved by, and I was convinced that I was not in the way of heaven, but in the way to hell. This state I laboured under for the space of five or six months. The more I heard or read the more I [saw that I] was condemned as a sinner before God till at length I was brought to perceive that my life hung by a

slender thread, and if it was the will of God to cut me off at that time, I was sure I should be found in hell, as sure as God was in heaven. I saw my condemnation in my own heart, and I found no way wherein I could escape the damnation of hell, only through the merits of my dying Lord and Savior Jesus Christ; which caused me to make intercession with Christ, for the salvation of my poor immortal soul. . . .[13]

Liele made known his acceptance of Jesus Christ and his desire for complete faithfulness to the will of God, as was required by the Baptist faith. It was clear to those around him that he had abilities as a preacher, and he was encouraged to exercise them by ministering to both whites and Africans.

The historical origin of the Silver Bluff congregation founded by Liele is far from certain—it is usually dated between 1773 and 1775, although the cornerstone claims a date of 1750.[14] What is more certain is that the Silver Bluff Church was forced to disband due to the Revolutionary War. David George, manager of the church, and other members sought freedom with the British in Savannah. This move resulted in the formation of the First African Church of Savannah (also called First Church) led by Andrew Bryan and Jesse Peters. According to the historical account: "the progress of religion may only seem slow when, in 1788, about three years after the visit of Rev. Thomas Burton, they were again visited by Abraham Marshall, of Kioke, accompanied by a young preacher of color, named Jesse Golphin. Mr. Marshall baptized forty-five more of the congregation in one day, and on the 20th of January, 1788, organized them into a church, and ordained Mr. Bryan to the ministry as their pastor, with full authority to preach the gospel and administer the ordinances of Christ."[15] Two years after its founding, First African Church of Savannah was admitted to the Georgia Association of Baptist Churches and remained a part of this association until it became involved in the Savannah Association in 1803. When the membership of First Church reached roughly eight hundred, it was decided that the congregation should be divided, and Second African Baptist Church was founded in 1802.

This was just the beginning of First Church's role in the spread of African Baptist congregations. For example, after the end of slavery, the church sent young preachers to work with the recently freed slaves and to plant *praise houses* in Georgia.[16] During the early 1800s, African Baptist churches also developed in other southern states, including Kentucky, Tennessee, Alabama, Mississippi, and Louisiana. Outside the Deep South, historians note the emergence of black Baptist churches in Virginia as early as 1774; Massachusetts as of 1805; Pennsylvania in 1809; New Jersey in 1812; Manhattan in 1808; and Brooklyn in 1847. These are just a few examples of independent black Baptist communities during the years prior to the Civil War. The appeal of these relatively independent black churches—some making use of white ministers—is clear in that participation in such a church was a step toward complete personhood and freedom in an oppressive land. These churches and others like them functioned as best they could under existing social restrictions. Fear that such gatherings would result in rebellions, combined with growing pressure on slaveholders from northern abolitionists, made the development of independent black Baptist associations impossible. One example of the realization of this apprehension of insurrection was the rebellion organized by Baptist minister Nat Turner in 1831. Turner was born into slavery thirty-one years earlier with markings that, according to folk wisdom, signaled great abilities and a profound destiny. Impressive intellectual abilities exhibited as a child only reinforced the opinion that Turner had been selected by God for a special purpose. For many of the more religious on the plantation, this special purpose was spoken of in terms of ministry.

Turner was drawn to scripture that focused on the coming of justice through judgment, and he came to believe that God had appointed him to bring about judgment on those who perpetuated the system of slavery. Always mindful of this sense of calling, Turner could not find peace in escaping and securing his own freedom. Visions convinced him that he had been appointed to preach the gospel and to bring freedom: "and on the appearance of the sign [the eclipse of the sun in February 1831] I should arise and prepare myself, and slay my enemies with their own weapons. And immediately on the sign appearing in the heavens, the seal was removed from my lips, and I communicated the great work laid out for me to do, to four in whom I had the greatest confidence. It was intended by us to have begun the work of death. . . ."[17] Turner perceived a solar eclipse as a necessary sign from God in February 1831, but illness kept him from beginning the mission on July 4 as planned. In August, Turner received another sign—a strange coloration of the sky—and began his work of "bringing death" to slaveholders. From midnight on Sunday,

August 21, until Tuesday morning, Turner and those with him battled whites in the surrounding area, leaving over 120 slaves and whites dead. Unable to complete his task, Turner escaped into the woods only to be found and eventually hung for leading the insurrection.

This rebellion and others like it resulted in resistance to Christianization of slaves by many slaveholders who did not want religion to turn their slaves into Nat Turners. Maintenance of the slave system meant securing the dominance of whites above all else. Circumstances for African Baptists grew even worse when white Baptists underwent a North-South split over the issue of slavery. In short, those opposed to slavery questioned the right of slaveholding Baptists to serve as missionaries: could one who held others in bondage provide a proper witness to the Gospel of Christ? Friction over this issue resulted in the formation of the Southern Baptist Convention in 1845 and the Baptist Missionary Union, which handled missionary activities for northern Baptists.

The rather inconsistent conversion rate of enslaved Africans to the Baptist faith resulted from a combination of factors, including inconsistent access to plantations, legal restrictions on the gathering of slaves, and internal conflict over the issue of slavery within Baptist circles. After all, Baptists had a tenacious hold on the idea of individual freedom, but did this freedom apply to blacks? By extension, was the holding of slaves a sin? Theological questions such as these were addressed in light of material objectives of southern Baptist slaveholders. This was not a balanced debate. The material objectives and existing social conventions often won out, producing as a by-product questionable missionary practices with less impressive results than might have been possible. Although the Civil War and Reconstruction would change some of this, it was not uncommon prior to 1865 for enslaved Africans to embrace the Baptist faith in spite of white Baptists. In many cases, African Baptists held a degree of independence in that their services were conducted with little supervision and monitoring from whites (as was required by law and social custom).

Notwithstanding race-based opposition, restrictions, and repression, the number of African Baptists continued to grow, reaching a total of forty thousand by 1813. This figure is rather small in light of the total African population of the South, yet it is an impressive development from the less than twenty thousand black Baptists in the South only eighteen years earlier. Most of these southern converts had no choice but to remain in white churches or plantation missions until after the end of slavery, while some made use of rare opportunities to develop their own churches. The work of this latter group was impressive. According to some estimates there were over two hundred black Baptist churches before the end of the Civil War, mostly in the South, with a total membership of close to five hundred thousand.

In addition to this significant growth in the number of African Baptists in the South prior to Reconstruction, it is also important to note the opportunity for independent church bodies in the North. The work of bringing Africans into the Baptist fold often fell to devout persons such as Nathaniel Paul, who combined a concern for religious independence with a call for abolition. According to Paul:

> Slavery, with its concomitant and consequences, in the best attire in which it can possibly be presented, is but a hateful monster, the very demon of avarice and oppression, from its first introduction to the present time; it has been among all nations the scourge of heaven, and the curse of the earth. It is so contrary to the laws which the God of nature has laid down as the rule of action by which the conduct of man is to be regulated towards his fellow man, which binds him to love his neighbour as himself, that it ever has, and ever will meet the decided disapprobation of heaven."[18]

This perspective advocated by Paul was held by many Africans in the North, and it became a major platform for Baptist churches, including Paul's Hamilton Street Baptist Church in Albany, New York, and Abyssinian Baptist Church in New York City (1808). The efforts of these churches were extremely important, but it was understood that a much more expansive effort was necessary, one that encompassed larger geographic areas in both the North and the South.

Church collectives were important because they allowed local churches to think and act beyond their own walls, which helped start missions and also better the fate of Africans in more substantive ways. The situation in the North was far from perfect, but it was liberal enough to allow for the organizing of the first collective of African Baptists, which was called the American Baptist Missionary Convention, founded at New York City's Abyssinian Baptist Church in 1849. The harsh nature of race relations in the South before and after Reconstruction made the formation of African alliances there more dangerous, if not impossible. In the West, however, circumstances made possible the development of all-black Baptist associations as early as 1834 in Ohio (the Providence Baptist Association), followed by associations in Illinois and Michigan.[19] When associations formed, they tended to embrace abolitionist views, which was often evident in their names. For example, the Union Anti-Slavery Baptist Association was founded in 1843 with thirteen churches and one thousand members. In fewer than thirty years, it grew to sixty-eight churches with a total membership close to five thousand. For some associations, this concern with abolitionism was tied to missions. This was the case with the development of missionary societies such as the Colored Baptist Home Missionary Society in Illinois (1844) as well as a short-lived expansion of this organization named the Western Colored Baptist Convention (1853–59).[20] Other regional conventions formed during this period include the General Association of the Western States and Territories (1873); the New England Baptist Missionary Convention (1874); and the Missionary Baptist State Convention of Tennessee, North Alabama, North Mississippi, East Arkansas, and Kentucky (1875). Other mission-focused organizations included the Baptist Foreign Mission Convention (1880), which sought to coordinate the foreign and domestic mission efforts of regional and local associations.

Ministers and laity alike took the formation of conventions as an opportunity to articulate a commitment to freedom with more power than could be mustered by any single congregation. For the Western Colored Baptist Convention, for example, this anti-slavery thrust was expressed in two resolutions approved in 1854: "Resolved, That we deeply sympathize with our enslaved brethren, and will do all that we can morally and politically, to relieve them from their thraldom. . . . [And be it resolved] that we still continue to declare ourselves bound by the ties of common brotherhood, to do all we can for the general good of mankind."[21] Although the activism in these various conventions was not without debate, what was always clear was a commitment to social change. What was less certain was the proper mode of activism.

Recognizing the value of cooperative action, an effort was made to further consolidate conventions through the development of statewide conventions able to act on the mission impulse of churches in even more far-reaching ways. These regional collectives were followed by attempts to organize African Baptists beyond state-based associations for the purpose of advancing spiritual and educational concerns. One such attempt is noteworthy because it marks the first push toward a national organization. In 1866, the Northwestern and Southern Baptist Convention (organized in 1864 in Saint Louis, Missouri) and the American Baptist Missionary Convention (founded in 1840 at the Abyssinian Baptist Church) united to form the Consolidated American Baptist Missionary Convention, with William Troy of Richmond, Virginia, as its president. Two years later, reports put membership at one hundred thousand. Within three years of its founding, the convention contained almost seventy-five churches and more than a dozen associations. Leading members of the convention argued that its resources should be used to help the recently freed in the South, but such efforts would not come without trouble. The convention recognized that resistance existed: "Brethren, we are watched. We are not accepted as a body or denomination qualified to manage our own missionary and educational work, and many of those who most discredit our capacity . . . have set themselves up as our benefactors, and call upon our friends to aid us through them. But our very organization is our proclamation to the world that we are able to do this work, and that we ought to do it."[22]

The period between the Civil War and the end of Reconstruction (1877), the time during which many of these conventions formed, marked a time of tremendous growth for Baptist churches. This growth, resulting in large part from the efforts of missionaries such as Edmund Kelly, Sampson White, and Israel Campbell, did not come without internal questioning of the Baptist agenda and method: Should Baptists concentrate on domestic missions to the exclusion of foreign concerns? Do African American Baptists make the best missionary representatives among the recently freed? Most agreed that priority must be given to the southern mission field and that as many African American missionaries as possible must lead the work. Yet, it was more difficult to secure consensus on two other issues: (1) class-based questions revolving around the appropriateness of folk religion and practices within Baptist church worship; and (2) the church's best response to social attitudes and political agendas on the national level. Concerning the first issue, missionaries in the South found themselves confronted with cultural ways that ran contrary to their northern sensibilities, and in too many instances they responded with an attitude of paternalism and superiority. For example, some objected to the singing of spirituals as opposed to more "refined" forms of music. This attitude led to conflict between these missionaries and local preachers, and the northern bias of missionary-sponsoring organizations only provided a further irritant. Nonetheless, representatives of black-run religious organizations provided the recently freed with an option of greater self-determination and autonomy that many found acceptable, regardless of the nagging classist and political conflicts.

Many white Baptists were troubled by the strong show of independence represented by the development of conventions. It reminded them that slavery and its restraints had come to an end. Needless to say, many fought these social and religious changes by physically attacking black churches, as well as relying on more subtle types of intimidation. Thus, the formation of churches, associations, and conventions, even when short-lived, offered a much-needed degree of spiritual and material autonomy.

The strength of sectional interests, fueled by this prevailing attitude of autonomy that marked Baptist congregations, resulted in the demise of the Consolidated American Baptist Convention between 1878 and 1879. The autonomy enjoyed by Baptist churches was a mixed blessing in that it guaranteed freedom for local congregations regardless of size but also made compromise difficult on issues like mission agendas, financial arrangements, and other workings of associations and conventions. This dilemma meant perpetual schisms and reorganizations. The problem facing local churches as well as associations and conventions is illustrated by the workings of the Baptist Foreign Mission Convention mentioned above. This convention's relationship with white Baptists was more problematic than beneficial. Yet some African American Baptists were still hopeful about working across racial lines while others pushed for complete independence. Both camps were present in the Baptist Foreign Mission Convention, which resulted in a great deal of infighting as well as the eventual formation of another convention in 1886, the American National Baptist Convention, with William J. Simmons as its president. The main objective of this new convention was to unify the church on these pressing racial issues.

Debate over the most effective means to achieve mission objectives was not the only cause of schisms. In 1893, debate over educational opportunities for Baptist ministers resulted in the founding of the National Baptist Education Convention. Its objective was to promote the development of an educated and trained clergy capable of leading Baptists in the achievement of their agenda of racial uplift.

◆

In summary, the development of the Baptist Church stems directly from conflict over the nature of baptism. Some members of the Church of England eventually broke away because they (Separatists) argued that baptism was only appropriate for adults because they alone were capable of confessing faith in Jesus Christ. Those who held this perspective began developing churches in England and not long after in North America. With time, Baptists in North America formed clearly defined subgroups and, although each group was concerned with spreading the Gospel of Christ, the Separate Baptists were particularly revival-minded. While their work brought many whites into the Baptist faith, the revivals also resulted in the conversion of many Africans. As early as the 1700s black Baptist churches began to develop in the South. With time, these separate congregations worked together to develop associations and conventions that allowed them to combine resources earmarked for the religious and material needs of Africans in America. Like their Methodist counterparts, Baptist churches experienced tremendous growth during the Civil War and Reconstruction. But unlike Methodists, they were unable to place this work within the context of a national organization until the nineteenth century.

Study Questions

1. What sparked the development of Baptist churches in England and North America?
2. What were the various groups of Baptists present in North America by the nineteenth century and what doctrinal differences mark them?
3. What attracted Africans to Baptist churches during the eighteenth and nineteenth centuries?
4. When and why do associations and conventions form within African Baptist circles?
5. What prevented the formation of a national Baptist organization prior to 1895?

National Baptist Convention, U.S.A., Inc.

Baptists worked to balance autonomy and cooperation to benefit their shared concern with both foreign and domestic missions. What resulted, in 1895, was the formation of the National Baptist Convention, U.S.A., Inc., based on a merger of three religious bodies—the Baptist Foreign Mission Convention of the United States of America, the American National Baptist Convention, and the National Baptist Educational Convention of the U.S.A. The new convention took as its mission not only the promotion of spiritual health among the recently freed slaves but also the development of skills and attitudes necessary to claim full humanity and act accordingly. Elias Camp Morris was elected the first president of the convention. Morris was a pastor from Arkansas, where he helped found the Arkansas Baptist College, so his organizational skills were highly valued in starting up this fledgling convention.

This convention harnessed the energy and resources of more African American Christians than any other denomination, which helped create public space in which African Americans could achieve their educational, cultural, and social goals. Even political ideas and objectives were discussed and debated in church halls and pulpits. The development of this first national convention also allowed Baptists to undertake these activities beyond the regional level. In this way, they fostered a national discourse on issues of great importance to the welfare of African Americans. For example, it provided a space for thinking about identity—what it meant to be African American—in complex and textured ways.[23] In short, the convention afforded an opportunity to develop black consciousness within the context of a scriptural call for justice and equality.

With both foreign and domestic mission boards and a publishing house by 1897, the convention sought to continue the Baptist goal of uplifting African Americans through strategies and programs that operated independently of white involvement. One would think the growing hostility toward African Americans expressed through formal laws and extra-legal mob activities would result in the strengthening of Baptist solidarity as a way of safeguarding the interest of African Americans. However, in spite of this reason for unity, the national convention experienced a schism resulting in the formation of the Lott Carey Baptist Home and Foreign Mission Convention at

Calvin Scott Brown

Shiloh Baptist Church in Washington, D.C. The first president of this convention was C. S. Brown. Briefly stated, the reasons for this split revolved around the planned relocation of the Foreign Mission Board's headquarters from Richmond to Louisville and the friction created over the complete rejection by some of cooperative ventures with the white American Baptist Publication Society. Those interested in cooperation with whites argued that this move, coupled with separatist publishing efforts, would be an unproductive break with white Baptist organizations and also jeopardize their livelihood through a loss of revenue as agents (for publications produced by these organizations). They also feared that the National Baptist Convention could not generate the income necessary to achieve its lofty goal of far-ranging missions.[24] Furthermore, they saw cooperation as a necessary sign of gratitude for white support in earlier years. The National Baptist Convention would later soften its position of complete separation from white Baptists through joint mission and educational efforts. But in 1897, based on these arguments, those who opposed complete independence left the convention and formed the Lott Carey Foreign Missionary Convention, named after one of the most important black Baptist missionaries of the nineteenth century.

In 1905, the two conventions formed an understanding based upon a proposal put forth a couple of years earlier. C. S. Brown stated that the proposal could only be acted upon if the National Baptist Convention was willing to make the following concessions related to the earlier points of friction:

> 1. A readjustment of our foreign mission work so as to heal the breach that produced our separation and a compromise of minor matters. 2. An agreement to refrain from unwarranted attacks on the officers of the American Baptist Home Mission Society and their work, and the adoption of a cooperation policy with the same when such action would strengthen the work among us. 3. An agreement to permit our Sunday Schools to use the literature of either publishing house without considering them loyal or disloyal, and also to permit the agents and representatives of either house or both houses to appear in our convention, associations, and other meetings, and be courteously received and entertained. 4. A decision to demand the officers of our general organization to refrain from slanderous assaults on brethren who dare to differ with them. 5. By conceding the supremacy of state bodies in all matters appertaining to the work within the respective jurisdictions.[25]

Once these concerns were addressed the two conventions entered into a relationship of cooperation on foreign missions.

The National Baptist Convention was attentive to the issue of "refining" African Americans in worship and social actions in order to bring them into the mainstream of American life. For example, Baptist missionaries sought to downplay the emotional elements of worship as a demonstration of overall sophistication. Some local ministers were offended by the assumption that their religious practices were not as important as those of the white folk. While many churches adopted the use of hymns and other elements of worship suggested by the missionaries, their worship ethos retained much of their traditional practices such as shouting. Baptists, of course, were not alone in wrestling with the nature of proper worship. The development of a trained professional clergy was a way of gaining the trust and support of a larger white society that viewed African Americans as uncultured barbarians. African American Methodists such as Henry McNeal Turner also raised questions concerning the use of spirituals, for example. But the strength of ties within Methodist denominations made uniformity in worship a different issue. Some members of the National Baptist Convention may have been troubled by this, but they also had to understand the need to maintain local autonomy, with all its ramifications related to worship style, as an essential component of Baptist practice.

The convention also developed educational opportunities that resulted in the foundation of numerous elementary and secondary schools as well as colleges such as Shaw University and Morehouse College. In addition to domestic education initiatives, the convention supported the development of educational opportunities on mission fields in Africa. This work in education, however, was coupled with public protest against discrimination in labor, housing, and employment. Betterment of the conditions in Africa was understood as an international concern when one took into consideration the various missionary efforts underway in the nineteenth century. For example, Lott Carey became the first black Baptist missionary to Africa in 1821, when he began work in Liberia. Even earlier, Prince Williams served as a missionary to the Bahamas (1777), and George Liele, who helped found Silver Bluff Church, organized a Baptist church in Kingston, Jamaica (1784). Since these events, Baptist churches through their conventions have extended missionary efforts by providing religious

and educational instruction and health care to people in Africa, India,
the Caribbean, and South America.

National Baptist Convention, U.S.A., Inc., Timeline

1894 *National Baptist Magazine* first published

1895 National Baptist Convention, U.S.A., formed

1895 National Baptist Foreign Mission Board developed

1897 Publishing Board incorporated

1897 Convention members demand complete separation from
Northern Baptist Societies

1897 Schism results in the Lott Carey Baptist Home and Foreign
Mission Convention

1899 National Baptist Young Peoples Union organized

1900 Women's Convention formed

1901 United American Free Will Baptist Church developed

1905 Relationship between Lott Carey and National Baptist forged

1906 National Primitive Baptist Convention founded

1908 Publishing Board begins building church furniture

1909 Publishing Board develops National Baptist Teacher-Training
Service

1921 National Baptist Evangelical Life and Soul-Saving Assembly of
the U.S.A. founded

1939 Dr. L. K. Williams gives a speech at the World's Fair in
New York

1941 D. V. Jemison elected president during the sixty-first
Annual Session

1956 Symposium titled "National Baptists Facing Integration:
Shall Gradualism Be Applied?" held to discuss the best approach
to social transformation

1958 Convention votes to give Joseph H. Jackson a life term as
president

1960 Baptist sit-in at the eightieth annual session

1961 Nannie Helen Burroughs dies

1965 Trudy Trimm becomes first female pastor accepted in the
convention

Because affiliation with conventions was voluntary and participation in no way compromised local church autonomy, efforts to unite
all Baptists would continuously fail, resulting in a variety of schisms.
Besides those already mentioned, numerous other breaks took place,
resulting in the formation of the United American Free Will Baptist

Church (1901) and the National Primitive Baptist Convention (1906), for example. In all, since 1895, there have been more than ten national conventions formed. Various efforts have been made to merge conventions but with little success. For example, efforts to unite the Lotty Carey Foreign Missionary Convention and the National Baptist Convention failed in 1905. This action was followed by two schisms (1915 and 1961) within the National Baptist Convention. Conflict over the National Baptist Convention's publishing board caused the 1897 schism as well as the 1915 split. Before the second schism, the National Baptist Convention had roughly three million members and some twenty thousand churches. The National Baptist Convention, U.S.A., Inc., remained, even after this split, the major black Baptist convention, with over five million members by the 1960s.

From Reconstruction through World War I, the National Baptist Convention advocated self-sufficiency for African Americans. Ministers of this convention pushed education, temperance, and other forms of social respectability as a way of gaining a greater role in the life of the nation. From their perspective, all other institutions (such as businesses and banks) should see the Black Church as a starting point and source of support for their ventures. The convention's president, E. C. Morris, argued that the church was the centerpiece of the African American community, which would instill in African Americans the moral compass necessary for full participation in society. Furthermore, through their example, African American Christians would inspire white Americans to act with tolerance and a commitment to equality.[26]

Baptist conventions and Methodist denominations shared a common struggle with the recognition of the importance of women for religious life and ministry. But whereas Methodist churches eventually recognized that the talents of black women extend into ordained ministry, Baptist Conventions have made no such turnabout. It is true that there are black women pastoring in the various conventions, particularly since the 1970s, but this does not point to a general tolerance. Historian Evelyn Brooks Higginbotham has helped to rethink Baptist history in light of the work done by the women of the African American Baptist conventions. As she notes, without their fundraising abilities, work as missionaries, and activities through women's conventions and clubs, Baptist conventions would have been hard-pressed to meet the needs of changing African American communities.

The Women's Convention of the National Baptist Convention was formed in 1900 through the efforts of Nannie Helen Burroughs and others. Serving as an umbrella organization for regional women's departments, the Women's Convention committed itself to ministry beyond the walls of the black church. While these women did not technically give sermons, they did give speeches and lectures across the country in which they outlined the high moral and ethical standards necessary for racial uplift. In keeping with popular appeals to social conformity as the way to gain acceptance in the United States, the Women's Convention promoted schools and settlement houses as training grounds for good citizens. In undertaking these projects and challenging traditional notions of what women ought to be, "they rejected a model of womanhood that was fragile and passive, just as they deplored a type preoccupied with fashion, gossip, or self-indulgence. They argued that women held the key to social transformation, and thus America offered them a vast mission field in which to solicit as never before the active participation of self-disciplined, self-sacrificing workers."[27] This attitude defined the motivation of many women within Baptist conventions who, despite restrictions imposed on them, kept church doors open. In the words of Nannie Helen Burroughs: "The encroachments we had to tolerate before the war and during the war are pardoned, but we live at the high-noon of the brightest day of liberty of soul and body. God help us to so live that we may raise the standard higher and higher until the name 'Negro woman' will be a synonym for uprightness of character and loftiness of purpose. Let character, and not color, be the first requisite to admission into any home, church, or social circle, and a new day will break upon ten million people."[28]

Nannie Helen Burroughs
(Courtesy of Library of Congress LC-USZ62-79903)

With the work done by both men and women within Baptist circles, this convention grew and engaged in both domestic and international programs. To support the efforts of such a massive organization, the convention's infrastructure includes various boards, auxiliaries, and officers. With the presidency of Joseph H. Jackson (1953–82), the National Baptist Convention, U.S.A., Inc., moved from nine boards and commissions responsible for its internal operations, foreign operations, and domestic concerns to twenty-two such divisions (for example, Christian education and foreign missions). Each board is composed of representatives from each state as well as eight at-large members, and the board so composed is free to develop its agenda and all regulations necessary to meet this agenda. Officers of the convention include the president, a vice president for each state represented in the convention, five convention-wide vice presidents, a general secretary, four assistant secretaries, a treasurer, a statistician, a historiographer, an executive editor, and a convention attorney. With respect to overall governance, the convention is guided by a fifteen-member board of directors and a nine-member executive committee. Unlike Methodist churches, which are bound to a church hierarchy culminating in the general conference, local Baptist churches are under no obligation to participant in or be guided by the workings of its national organization and the board of directors.

◆

In summary, despite several earlier attempts, Baptists did not succeed in developing a national organization until 1895, when three regional conferences joined forces to form the National Baptist Convention, U.S.A. Using its ability to reach much farther than smaller conventions and individual churches, this convention concerned itself with the spiritual health and social development of African Americans. Two years after its formation, it had a foreign and domestic missions department as well as a publishing house. Based on voluntary association with the convention, local churches worked together to increase the reach of Baptist missions through the formation of schools and other outlets associated with racial uplift. This relationship, however, was not free from problems, and church leaders and members fought over the proper relationship with white Baptist organizations, among other issues. Internal feuds ultimately resulted in numerous schisms, which resulted in the National Baptist Convention of America (1915) and the Progressive National Baptist Convention (1961). But even with these developments, the National Baptist Convention, U.S.A., Inc., maintains its presence in black communities across the country as the largest African American denomination in the country.

Selected Leaders of the National Baptist Convention, U.S.A., Inc.

Nannie Helen Burroughs (1878–1961). Burroughs was born in Virginia but raised in Washington, D.C. After attending the famous M Street High School there, Burroughs sought employment as a teacher and city clerk but without success. In 1900, she moved to Kentucky where she became secretary for the Foreign Mission Board of the National Baptist Convention. From this position, Burroughs taught courses on domestic issues and developed the Woman's Industrial Club, which fed African Americans working in downtown Louisville. In addition to this work, Burroughs played a role in founding the Woman's Convention in 1900, an organization through which women could play a larger role in the National Baptist Convention's racial uplift efforts. When the Woman's Convention met for the first time in 1901, Burroughs appeared as its corresponding secretary. Her work on behalf of the Woman's Convention gave her a national reputation as a powerful speaker. Her abilities behind the lectern helped the convention raise money to start the National Training School for Women and Girls in 1909. In addition to her work with the Woman's Convention, Burroughs was an active participant in the Club movement of the early twentieth century through which African American women pushed issues of sociopolitical and economic concern.

Sutton Elbert Griggs (1872–1933). Griggs was born in Texas and received his education there prior to attending Richmond Theological Seminary in Virginia. After graduating from seminary in 1893, Griggs entered the pastorate and served congregations in Virginia and Tennessee. While pastor of First Baptist Church in Nashville, he was named corresponding secretary of the National Baptist Convention. In addition to his duties as a pastor and national officer, Griggs wrote books that countered the stereotypical and racist depictions of

African Americans found in much of the literature of his day. In 1899 he published *Imperium in Imperio,* which is considered the first protest novel written and published by an African American. This was followed in 1905 by a novel, *The Hindered Hand,* that responds to Thomas Dixon's *The Leopard's Spot* and *The Klansman,* which depicts African Americans as brutes and justifies mob violence against them. This book was followed by *One Great Question: A Study of Southern Conditions at Close Range.* Griggs combined his church work and protest novels with political engagement through the Niagara movement organized by W. E. B. DuBois. He would eventually modify his protest strategy and move from the pastorate to the National Religious and Civic Institute, which he founded in 1932.

WILLIAM HENRY JERNAGIN (1869–date unknown). Jernagin was born in Mississippi. Prior to being licensed to preach, Jernagin served as a teacher in his home. In 1892 he was ordained and began pastoral work at Baptist churches in Mississippi and Oklahoma. In addition to working at the local level, he played a pivotal role in the development of the Young People's Christian Educational Congress of Mississippi and the Oklahoma General Baptist Convention. While a pastor in Washington, D.C., Jernagin was elected president of the National Race Congress and used this position to present his views to an international audience. In 1926, ten years after becoming president of the National Race Congress, Jernagin became head of the National Sunday School and Baptist Young People's Union Congress of America. While holding this position, he also served as president of the Consolidated National Equal Rights League and Race Congress, among other public positions. Through his work, Jernagin enhanced the public profile of the National Baptist Convention and helped advance African Americans.

S. WILLIE LAYTEN (date unknown–1950). Although nothing is known about Layten's birthplace and youth, she is well known as the first president of the Woman's Convention founded in 1900 with Nannie H. Burroughs as corresponding secretary. Her many years of service in this capacity greatly increased the visibility of the Woman's Convention. In addition to the Woman's Convention's support of the National Training School, it also provided personnel and financial resources necessary to accomplish much needed missions.

ELIAS CAMP MORRIS (1855–1922). Morris was born into slavery in Georgia. After a conversion experience, he was licensed to preach and, five years later, he was ordained at nineteen years of age. Morris spent his career as a minister at Centennial Baptist Church in Arkansas. As pastor of this church, Morris became an important figure in the larger religious community and was elected secretary of the state convention only one year after arriving at the church. Moving through the ranks quickly, he became president of the convention and played a major role in founding Arkansas Baptist College. Morris's ministry was noted outside Arkansas and this resulted in him becoming president of the American National Baptist Convention. When this convention merged with two others and formed the National Baptist Convention, Morris was elected its first president.

Study Questions

1. How did the National Baptist Convention, U.S.A., Inc., form?
2. What is the structure of the convention?
3. What is the convention's mission?
4. What caused the schisms experienced by the convention?
5. What role have women played in the mission of the convention?

Suggested Reading

Harvey, Paul. *Redeeming the South: Religious Cultures and Racial Identities among Southern Baptists, 1865–1925*. Chapel Hill: University of North Carolina Press, 1997. This text provides an insightful discussion of the development of Baptist churches, with a sensitivity to the racial and class factors that influenced the religious terrain of the southern states.

Higginbotham, Evelyn Brooks. *Righteous Discontent: The Women's Movement in the Black Baptist Church, 1880–1920*. Cambridge: Harvard University Press, 1993. Higginbotham provides one of the most important studies of the involvement of women in the National Baptist Convention. It should be essential reading for anyone interested in the development of Baptist churches in African American communities.

Jackson, Joseph H. *A Story of Christian Activism: The History of the National Baptist Convention, U.S.A., Inc.* Nashville: Townsend, 1980.

This text provides an insider perspective on the history of the National Baptist Convention, written by one of its more controversial presidents.

Jordan, Lewis G. *Negro Baptist History, U.S.A., 1750–1930.* Nashville: Sunday School Publishing Board, 1930. This is a fairly early study of the Baptist Conventions in African American communities, which should be read along with less celebratory treatments.

The official homepage for the National Baptist Convention, U.S.A., Inc., is www.nationalbaptist.org.

National Baptist Convention of America

Prior to 1915, Richard Boyd was secretary of the National Convention's Publishing Board, which was incorporated in his name, and was responsible for much of the board's early success through the building of a new physical plant on land he donated to the convention. In keeping with Booker T. Washington's philosophy, Boyd believed African Americans must help themselves through the development of institutions with economic power and authority. He exercised this belief by developing personal business opportunities as well as increasing the convention's publishing concerns. In 1896, Boyd had the Publishing Board chartered. After some controversy, the advisory board that he developed to monitor the publishing activities gained the approval of the convention. The creation of the board, however, gave rise to conflict over how boards should be managed by the convention. The president of the convention, E. C. Morris, sensed that Boyd's control over the convention's publishing ventures posed a problem, and he acted to separate the publishing house from the Home Mission Board.

For many members of the convention, the strong independence that Boyd and his board continued to demonstrate foreshadowed a move toward autonomy from the convention. For example, Boyd's stance concerning cooperation with white Baptists troubled many members of the convention. Boyd published materials that saw African Americans in a positive light and destroyed stereotypical depictions often found in the literature coming from white Baptists.[29]

In order to secure this freedom from destructive representations, he argued that black Baptists had to develop the capacity to produce their own materials. Although concerned with African American self-sufficiency, Boyd was willing to cooperate with white Baptists, such as James M. Frost of the Sunday School Board of the Southern Baptist Convention. He argued, however, that this cooperation had to be premised on equality not dependence. In his words: "The National Baptist Convention has a right to own and control its own business enterprises, to maintain, on a larger scale, distinctive educational institutions, and in the exercise of this priestly prerogative, no band of white brethren anywhere should undertake to embarrass or molest them. With the recognition of these rights and corresponding brotherly treatment, our white brethren will find in the constituency of the National Baptist Convention *ardent friends* and *loyal supporters*" (italics in original).[30] The materials published under Boyd's leadership were extremely popular, and they resulted in the Publishing Board becoming successful enough to venture into the production and distribution of other goods used within churches (such as furniture). Boyd enjoyed the success of the board and found it difficult to surrender control over its activities. He argued that the board's affiliation with the convention did not give the latter authority over the former. As one might expect, this position created a good deal of resentment.

Morris was concerned that Boyd held undue influence over the Publishing Board, which could easily result in an "oligarchy in Baptist Institutions."[31] This, of course, destroyed lines of authority, within a church structure, that were already fragile. In response to this fear, Morris and his supporters demanded that Boyd provide financial records demonstrating that funds were not being misused. This move by Morris caused a rift that forced convention ministers into one of two camps: pro-Boyd or pro-Morris. Boyd and others objected to Morris's move and court action ended in Boyd's favor because the Publishing Board was incorporated in his name. He argued that the National Baptist Convention's constitution did not mention the development of a publishing concern. Hence, his work related to publishing was a matter of private activity that had never received much support from the convention. From his perspective, the convention's demands related to the publishing house were an indefensible power play.

Continuing friction resulted in the formation of another convention, at Salem Baptist Church in Chicago, first known as the National

Baptist Convention, Unincorporated, which was later referred to as the National Baptist Convention of America. According to historian Milton Sernett, "most delegates who withdrew under the banner of the National Baptist Convention, Unincorporated, were from Texas and Arkansas. The rival national bodies fought over the state conventions and regional associations, and uncertainty prevailed regarding the number of members and churches allied with Boyd and his camp."[32] What is certain, however, is that this schism fostered a sense of mistrust among Baptists resulting in continued friction. Furthermore, the dislike between these two conventions made it extremely difficult to act on the mission zeal voiced prior to 1915.

National Baptist Convention of America Timeline[33]

1896 Richard Boyd outlines his strategy for the National Baptist Convention's Publishing Board

1905 Convention seeks to separate the management of the Home Mission Board and the Publishing Board, both ignore the request

1914 Rebellion against the 1905 requirement for separate management continues and pushes the convention to rethink the relationship between the convention and the various boards

1915 Issues around the Publishing Board result in a court case centered around Boyd and Morris

1915 National Baptist Convention of America formed

1916 New convention publishes a document explaining its position called "The Rightful and Lawful Ownership of the National Baptist Publishing House"

1916 Constitution of the convention amended

1917 Constitution adopted

1924 Lott Carey and the new convention cooperate on foreign missions concerns

1928 Convention incorporates its Foreign Mission Board, Baptist Young People's Union, and Sunday School Publishing Board

1928 The American Baptist Theological Seminary and the National Training School for Women and Girls in Washington, D.C., are incorporated

1930s New convention is incorporated

1940 Wendell Clay Somerville becomes president of the convention and is credited by many for revitalizing it

Efforts were made to heal the conflict between the two conventions, but these attempts did not result in unification. The National Baptist Convention of America, however, was able to develop links in 1925 with the Lott Carey Baptist Foreign Mission Convention with respect to a shared interest in foreign missions. Over the years, however, this foreign mission cooperation declined.

After this schism, the Southern Baptist Convention—with which the National Baptists had hoped to work—continued its efforts toward joint activities with the National Baptist Convention, U.S.A., Inc., but African American Baptists found it difficult to cooperate long enough to enact effective mission strategies. Their struggle over church boards and auxiliaries occupied too much time, and the Great Migration only added to their organizational struggles by shifting convention membership from South to North while reducing financial resources. Put another way, "clergy with scattered or weakened congregations no longer had regular salaries. The southern state associations, the principal source of mission contributions, were themselves in financial crisis. . . . The Boyd-led Baptists were also handicapped in their ability to address the institutional crisis precipitated by the Great Migration."[34] Even so, each president interpreted the new convention's concern with the social and spiritual issues facing African Americans and worked to improve the condition of this community.

The organizational structure of this convention is similar to that of the National Baptist Convention, U.S.A., Inc. Monitoring the activities of this convention and its more than two million members are sixteen national officers, including the president, three vice presidents, a series of associate vice presidents who are also the presidents of state conventions or moderators of the general associations, a recording secretary with four assistants; a corresponding secretary, a statistical secretary, a treasurer, an auditor, a director of public relations, a historian, and a secretary for youth activities. The executive board provides guidance for all of these officers. In addition to these units, the convention is also composed of five committees responsible for the financial and administrative activities of the convention and seven program boards that oversee missions, publications, evangelism, youth concerns, and charity. States are represented by these programs and boards, which allows the convention to remain sensitive to regional and local concerns and perspectives. Additional complexity is present in the workings of this convention through auxiliary units such as the Women's Missionary and Junior Women's auxiliaries and the Nurses' Corps as well as four commissions responsible for overseeing transportation, Christian education, social justice, and military ministry.[35]

◆

In summary, R. H. Boyd's leadership of the National Baptist Convention's Publishing Board troubled members of the convention, including president E. C. Morris. For many, Boyd exercised a degree of independence with respect to the board's agenda and activities that brought into question its relationship to the convention. This conflict escalated until it became necessary for the courts to decide the issue. The decision favored Boyd but it did not end the controversy. Feuding continued between the two camps—Boyd supporters and Morris supporters—until a schism was unavoidable. In 1915, Boyd and his supporters left the convention and formed the National Baptist Convention of America. With a similar sense of racial uplift and organizational structure as the National Baptist Convention, U.S.A., Inc., the new convention reached out to African Americans, increasing its membership and influence.

Selected Leaders of the National Baptist Convention of America

HENRY ALLEN BOYD (1876–1959). The son of Richard Boyd, Henry Boyd shared his father's interest in the Baptist Church and its business potential. He played a major role in running the various businesses his father developed as offshoots of the Publishing Board. With the death of his father in 1922, he assumed leadership of all divisions of the board's activities under the National Baptist Convention of America. Boyd was also instrumental in the development of the Tennessee Agricultural and Industrial State School (Tennessee State University).

RICHARD HENRY BOYD (1843–1922). Born a slave in Mississippi, Boyd (originally named Dick Gray) tried his hand at various occupations before entering the ministry. Although he did not learn to read and write until he was twenty-four, Boyd played a fundamental role in organizing a Baptist association in Texas. When the National Baptist

Convention was formed in 1895, Boyd became its secretary for Home Missions. In 1897 he founded the convention's Publishing Board. He was able to develop this board along with a variety of other businesses, such as the National Negro Doll Company (1911), which made African American dolls, and the One Cent Savings Bank and Trust in 1904. The Publishing Board was extremely successful and allowed the convention to produce its own materials, including documents that served the religious needs of African Americans while also countering negative depictions of African Americans found in popular press. Boyd's control over the Publishing Board became an issue for the convention. This ultimately ended in the formation of the National Baptist Convention of America to which Boyd moved the Publishing Board.

THEOPHILUS BARTHOLOMEW BOYD JR. (1917–71). Born in Nashville into a family deeply connected to the convention, Boyd held several positions within the convention's publishing plant after attending Fisk University and Tennessee A & I State College. Moving through the ranks, he learned all aspects of the publishing business and was eventually elected secretary-treasurer and chief administrator of the Publishing Board. During his administration, the board built a million-dollar structure to house all components of the publishing business.

CALVIN SCOTT BROWN (1859–194?). Born in North Carolina, Brown received his formal education from Shaw University where he earned the B.A. and B.D. degrees. Upon graduation, he moved to Winton, North Carolina, and was the pastor of a local church while also organizing the Waters Training School. By 1900, Brown had completed his education by earning two additional degrees, the D.D. and M.A. from Shaw University. Due to his concern with missions, Brown participated in the formation of the Lott Carey Baptist Foreign Mission Convention, which eventually became the foreign mission wing of the National Baptist Convention of America.

JAMES C. SAMS (1909–85). Born in Georgia, Sams spent his life as part of the Baptist Church. After receiving ordination at the age of twenty-one, he attended Florida A & M College. However, prior to receiving his degree, he served as pastor for a Florida congregation. Sams became a vice president of the convention and was eventually elected its president in 1967. From this position Sams influenced the workings of the church in foreign missions, among other areas, and built a national reputation for himself.

Study Questions

1. What was the source of conflict that spurred the formation of this convention?
2. What was R. H. Boyd's stance on cooperation with white Baptists?
3. What are the structural similarities between the two Baptist conventions discussed thus far?
4. How would you describe Boyd's position on the progress of African Americans? What were some of the ways that African Americans advanced in society?
5. What was the agenda of the National Baptist Convention of America during its early years?

Suggested Reading

Collier-Thomas, Bettye. *Daughters of Thunder: Black Women Preachers and Their Sermons, 1850–1979.* San Francisco: Jossey-Bass, 1998. This text provides brief historical and biographical context for black women preachers, including many within the Baptist Church.

Fitts, Leroy. *A History of Black Baptists.* Nashville: Broadman, 1985. This text is not limited to the National Baptist Convention of America; nonetheless, readers will find it a useful study of the development of all three conventions in light of socioeconomic, political, and religious questions and sensibilities.

Lincoln, C. Eric, and Lawrence H. Mamiya, *The Black Church in the African American Experience.* Durham: Duke University Press, 1990. This sociological study provides helpful information on all the major Baptist conventions as well as some sense of how they respond to pressing issues, such as the struggle to maintain the presence of young people.

We have been unable to locate a functioning site for this denomination. There is a site for the National Youth and Children's Convention: http://members.aol.com/nbyc1/index.html.

Progressive National Baptist Convention

Opposition to church involvement in the Civil Rights movement played a role in the eventual formation of the Progressive National Baptist Convention in 1961. However, the seeds for this break were planted much earlier and revolved around terms of service for the president of the National Baptist Convention, U.S.A., Inc. The issue of a maximum length of service as a constitutional issue first arose in 1952. During the 1956 annual session, a great deal of time was given to debating the findings of the tenure committee developed several years earlier to address length of service. The committee eventually suggested that all officers be subject to term limits. In 1957, several convention ministers took Joseph Harrison Jackson to court in an effort to prevent the overturning of the 1952 regulation. The federal court found in favor of Jackson and in payment for their efforts, Jackson had his opponents expelled from the convention.

Joseph H. Jackson (right, seated) assisting a family in need
(Courtesy of the Sunday School Publishing Board of the National Baptist Convention, U.S.A., Inc.)

For some, this move by Jackson pointed to a glaring problem within the convention: Jackson exercised too much power and had held this power for far too long. It was not simply a matter of power but also how this power was expressed. For many members of the convention, Jackson's increasingly conservative stance with respect to civil rights activities (underway as of the mid-1950s) posed a problem. Jackson was well aware of the racism strangling the efforts of

African Americans for advancement, and at times during his career he participated in protest activities. In fact, he recognized the demand for freedom as integral to the formation of the Baptist faith:

> The urge for freedom was one of the essential elements in that religious quest out of which the Baptist church historically evolved. Freedom was the motive, the objective, and the theme of that early group that finally became known as Baptists. When Roger Williams broke with the Massachusetts theocracy, he was not simply rebelling against order; rather he was impelled and inspired by the love of freedom. It was this same general spirit that captured the thinking and actions of the pioneers as well as those organizers of the National Baptist Convention. . . . The National Baptist Convention, U.S.A., Inc., is an organization of Americans who are believers in Christ, dedicated to His kingdom, and committed to first-class citizenship while maintaining firmly an anchor in the idea of the freedom of all mankind.[36]

Clearly, Jackson did not oppose change. Rather, he viewed Martin Luther King Jr.'s approach to change troubling because, from Jackson's perspective, King did not take seriously the importance of the U.S. Constitution and its democratic vision for social transformation. Furthermore, Jackson argued the convention had always encouraged its member churches to participate in programs geared toward individual liberty, civil rights, and human rights. He goes further to acknowledge the work done by members of the convention through the NAACP and the Southern Christian Leadership Conference.

> The National Baptist Convention is by origin, structure, and mission, a strictly religious body; but it is a religious body with concerns that relate it to human suffering, human needs, and human aspirations. Therefore, it is by nature related to the civil rights struggle. It has never insisted that other organizations devoted to civil rights accept its philosophy and work according to its policies and programs. It has shown its civil rights concern by working with other civil rights organizations and by taking responsibilities in the same field peculiar to its nature and its mission. It is therefore a helper of other organizations whose purposes include an unselfish service to mankind. The National Baptist Convention has supported the local branches of the NAACP as well as the national office. This support has continued and, in many ways, is on the increase.[37]

Jackson also points to the support of the Montgomery Bus Boycott by the convention. What Jackson objected to was the dismissal of gradualism by King and others. Jackson's opposition to King and the Civil Rights movement stifled the progressive posture desired by some members of the convention.

Gardner Taylor
(Courtesy of Baptist World Alliance)

In an effort to break Jackson's hold on the convention, several prominent members, including Martin Luther King Jr., Martin Luther King Sr., Ralph D. Abernathy, and Benjamin Mays, put Gardner Taylor's name forward as a candidate for the presidency during the 1960 meeting.[38] But in a move that troubled the "Taylor team," Jackson was nominated and quickly elected without consideration of Taylor's candidacy. When the Jackson camp made it clear that the election would not be reevaluated, those opposed to this move remained until after the end of the convention and then held another election with Taylor as the victor. The convention, of course, refused to acknowledge this second election, and the court case filed by the Taylor team failed to force Jackson out of office. As a consequence of this legal action, the convention punished ten leading members of this protest by removing them from the convention because of what they had "done against the rules of fellowship in opposition to and contrary to [its] principles and ideals."[39] Jackson's opponents regrouped and voiced their displeasure in September 1961 with this news release:

A Volunteer Committee for the Formation of a New National Baptist Convention announced this week through its Chairman, Rev. L. V. Booth, pastor of Zion Baptist Church, Cincinnati, Ohio, that a meeting will be held November 14 and 15, 1961, at Zion Baptist Church . . . . The two-day session will be devoted to discussion on How to Build a

Democratic Convention Dedicated to Christian Objectives. The keynote speaker will be Dr. William H. Borders, Pastor of Wheat Street Baptist Church, Atlanta, Georgia. Dr. Borders is one of the ten outstanding pastors expelled from the National Baptist Convention, Inc., following its notorious session at Louisville, Kentucky, in 1957, when President Joseph H. Jackson ruled Tenure unconstitutional. There has been great dissatisfaction since. . . . This movement is in no way connected with the past effort of "The Taylor Team." It is an entirely new movement under new leadership. Persons who are concerned with redeeming the Baptist initiative and restoring a Democratic Thrust are invited.[40]

With few alternatives and little hope for reconciliation in light of the friction generated by this second election and court case, those who had supported Taylor in 1960 met in Cincinnati only a few months after the above announcement and founded the Progressive National Baptist Convention. Those gathered represented more than twenty churches in fourteen states. Participants approached this meeting with urgency because "Our National Baptist Convention has reached an all-time low in fellowship, peace, and Christian dignity. We have completely lost our freedom to worship, participate and grow in the kingdom work as it is expressed in the Convention [National Baptist, Inc.]. We can no longer trust the integrity of its leadership. The time has come for freedom-loving, independent and peace-loving Christians to unite in a fellowship that they can trust."[41]

The new convention made T. M. Chambers its first president, with L. V. Booth as vice president; J. Carl Mitchell as secretary; Louis Rawls as treasurer; A. J. Hargett as director of publicity; and William W. Parker as the convention's attorney. The break with the National Baptist Convention was complete, and the Progressive National Baptist Convention quickly became involved in the Civil Rights movement and the anti-war efforts of the 1960s. In the words of the convention: "The onward march of time, the historical forwardness and the continuous renewal in time and history of God's revelations, cause the sensitive and alert souls to shake off the old forms and welcome new opportunities and new avenues of Christian service. . . . Inherent in the Progressive Concept is progress. We are going somewhere in the Progressive National Convention. We are done with the 'cult of personalities.' We are through with 'play prayers' and 'circus sermons.' . . . Progress is our theme word."[42] Although smaller than

---

Progressive National Baptist Convention Timeline

1952 National Baptist Convention, U.S.A., Inc., establishes term limits (tenure) for officers

1953 Joseph H. Jackson elected president of the convention

1955 Jackson offers the support of the convention to the Montgomery Bus Boycott

1956 Term limits debated during the annual session

1957 Lawsuit filed to prevent attempts to overturn the 1952 decision of the convention on the subject of term limits

1960 Pressure for new leadership in the convention becomes undeniable

1960 Effort made to get Gardner Taylor elected president of the convention

1960s Progressive National Baptist Convention plays major role in Civil Rights movement

1961 E. C. Estell reads a resolution requesting Jackson stand for reelection

1961 Ten ministers who opposed the reelection of Jackson are removed from their convention leadership positions

1961 Volunteer Committee for the Formation of a New National Baptist Convention announces a meeting to be held later that year

1961 Progressive National Baptist Convention formed

1962 Document written by W. H. R. Powell provides reasons for the new convention

1964 Martin Luther King Jr. receives the Nobel Peace Prize

1968 Martin Luther King Jr. assassinated

---

the two conventions already discussed, six years after its founding the Progressive National Baptist Convention claimed over a half million members in some 655 churches in the United States. The structure of the convention differs from that of the two larger Baptist conventions in that it is divided into four regions (South, Southwest, Midwest, and East), with state conventions in each region. It is composed of eight departments responsible for carrying out the convention's mission, including the Women's Department, Laymen's Department, Youth Department, and the Congress of Christian Education. In addition to these departments, there are various boards and commissions responsible for missions, publications, ministerial pensions, nonchurch-based ministries, convention arrangements, internal affairs, and economic development. Overseeing the workings of the convention is an array of officers similar to that of the two other conventions with one major distinction: all officers, including the president, are limited to two consecutive years of service.

◆

In summary, continued tension and conflict within the National Baptist Convention, U.S.A., Inc., resulted in a second major schism in 1961. The cause of this friction stems back to the issue of term limits for officers of the convention. In 1952, it had been decided that term limits should be observed. However, only five years after this, the president, Joseph H. Jackson, made an effort to have this regulation dismissed. Those who opposed this move nominated Gardner Taylor of Concord Baptist Church (New York) for the presidency. The failure of Jackson's supporters to take Taylor's candidacy seriously only deepened the conflict. When Jackson retained the presidency through both the workings of the convention and the legal system, his opponents began working out the plans for an alternate organization. In 1961, Taylor, Martin Luther King Jr., Martin Luther King Sr., and several others met and formed the Progressive National Baptist Convention. Beyond resolving conflict over term limits and leadership, the development of this new convention also freed Baptists to become involved in the Civil Rights movement, which Jackson had rejected.

Selected Leaders of the
Progressive National Baptist Convention

LAVAUGHN VENCHAEL BOOTH (1919–). Booth was born in Mississippi and received his education there prior to attending Howard University and the University of Chicago. After ordination, Booth pastored churches in Ohio and Indiana. Like Gardner Taylor, Martin Luther King Sr., and Martin Luther King Jr., he was frustrated by the convention's lack of energetic involvement in the Civil Rights movement. The initial meeting to organize the conference took place at his church, and he was elected vice president of the new convention. He would eventually serve as the convention's president. In addition to this post, Booth has also served as a member of the Martin Luther King Jr. Center board of directors as well as vice president of the Baptist World Alliance.

WILLIAM HOLMES BORDERS (1905–1993). Borders was born in Georgia. He received his formal education from Morehouse College, Garrett Theological Seminary, and the University of Chicago. During the course of Border's career, his ministry combined spiritual renewal with a concern for social transformation. The resources of his church in Evanston, Illinois, were used for various projects including the construction of a community center in 1954, which provided a full range of services. He also played a major role in securing employment for African Americans. Borders was involved in the actions that ultimately resulted in the desegregation of bus service and other public services. Furthermore, he spearheaded the creation of a 500-unit housing development, the first such structure in the United States.

TIMOTHY MOSES CHAMBERS (1895–1977). Born in Texas, Chambers received his education from Fort Worth I & M College and Bishop College. After being ordained, he served in a variety of posts, including president of the Baptist Missionary and Educational Convention and president of the Constitutional Baptist State Convention. Like Booth and several others, Chambers was troubled by the internal politics of the National Baptist Convention as well as its reluctance to take a lead in the civil rights struggle. When the schism occurred in 1961 resulting in the formation of the Progressive National Baptist Convention, Chambers was elected its first president.

MARTIN LUTHER KING SR. (1899–1984). King was born on a farm in Georgia but eventually left for Atlanta where he pursued educational opportunities and worked various jobs. Having been ordained in his home church (in Stockbridge), King, after a short time at East Point Baptist Church, organized Second Baptist Church. In 1931, after another pastorate of short duration, he became the pastor of Ebenezer Baptist church. As pastor of this church, King was involved in civil rights issues in Atlanta and gained a wide reputation as a leader. In addition to this work he also served for a time as moderator of the Atlanta Missionary Baptist Association.

GARDNER CALVIN TAYLOR (1918–). Born in Louisiana, Taylor had plans of becoming an attorney until he felt convinced God wanted him to enter ministry. He was ordained in 1939 and completed his ministerial training at Oberlin School of Theology the following year. Taylor was a pastor in Ohio and Louisiana before accepting the pastorate of Concord Baptist Church in Brooklyn, New York. Over the course of his time there, Taylor came to national attention and his church grew to be one of the largest in the country. He served as president of the Progressive National Baptist Convention shortly after its formation.

Study Questions

1. What motivated the formation of this convention?
2. How did its thought on social issues differ?
3. How does its structure differ from the other conventions?
4. What was this convention's stand on the Civil Rights movement?
5. Who were some of the major figures in its development?

Suggested Reading

Booth, William D. *The Progressive Story: New Baptist Roots.* Nashville: Townsend, 1981. This text provides a history of the Progressive National Baptist Convention from an insider's perspective.

Riggs, Marcia Y. *Can I Get a Witness?: Prophetic Religious Voices of African American Women: An Anthology.* Maryknoll, N.Y.: Orbis, 1997. This book contains speeches and sermons by prominent African American women, many of them Baptist.

Taylor, Clarence. *The Black Churches of Brooklyn.* New York: Columbia University Press, 1994. Concentrating on religious institutions in New York, readers will appreciate the manner in which Baptist churches are discussed within the context of other religious communities.

The official homepage for the Progressive National Baptist Convention is www.pnbc.org, and it provides brief historical information and links to other sites of interest.

CHAPTER 3

African American
Pentecostalism

The Development of the Holiness Movement

Anxiety over the spiritual condition of the United States dominated the thought of many evangelists during the late nineteenth century.[1] For example, Charles Price Jones, a minister who preached to enslaved Africans during the 1800s, promoted a sense of spiritual transformation that linked "salvation to the formation of character, which he envisioned as a more important foundation of society than family, politics, economic, or even the church."[2] Some of the more aggressive holders of this mindset took it upon themselves to spark a Holiness campaign that would enliven a devotion to God sorely missing in most Americans. This was a call to sanctification. Concisely stated, sanctification is individual holiness by which persons who have accepted Jesus Christ as their personal savior take another step in their spiritual lives involving cleansing from worldliness. *Salvation* is considered the first act of God's grace in that it is nothing the individual can earn or merit. *Sanctification, or holiness,* is thought of as a second act of God's grace by which the believer is brought into closer fellowship with God through the removal of sinfulness that separates us from God. This sinfulness includes improper attire and participation in secular forms of entertainment. In both the North and South, early advocates of Holiness wanted to move Christian churches beyond bourgeois sensibilities and secular concerns. The social and religious context giving rise to this Holiness push can be described, although not fully captured, this way:

The years that followed the Civil War were characterized by a moral depression in America. Returning soldiers with "battlefield ethics" entered not only the houses of business, but also the halls of government and the sanctuaries of the churches. Many of the younger recruits to the ministry entered their vocations with less training than their elders and less respect for the traditions and doctrines of the church. . . . Former customs such as the "mourner's bench" for penitent sinners, class meetings for the "perfection of the saints," and camp meetings for the benefit of both had been abandoned during the war.[3]

Despite prevailing customs, members of the Holiness movement, who were primarily Methodist in the beginning, understood real Christians to "be in the world but not of it." This doctrine came to be expressed in several different ways, but in general Holiness advocates wanted to return to the church of old and its major concern with righteousness in opposition to acceptance from worldly powers. Believing that the church could be redeemed and reformed, Holiness preachers and evangelists went about preaching their doctrine of entire sanctification or the second blessing of separation from worldliness.

For most scholars studying Holiness and Pentecostalism, an initial camp meeting at Vineland, New Jersey, in the 1860s represents an early and important marker of a powerful movement of religious excitement. Encouraged by the results of this camp meeting, a committee was developed and charged with keeping the movement alive by urging people to come to additional meetings: "Come, brothers and sisters of the various denominations, and let us in this forest-meeting, as in other meetings for the promotion of Holiness, furnish an illustration of evangelical union, and make common supplication for the descent of the Spirit upon ourselves, the church, the nation, and the world."[4] Over the course of the next sixteen years, more than fifty meetings were organized by this committee referred to as the National Camp Meeting Association for the Promotion of Holiness, or simply the National Holiness Association. These meetings were supplemented by written materials in various journals and newsletters that praised this push toward Holiness.

Through the energies of black evangelists such as Amanda Berry Smith, Levi Coppin, Benjamin Tanner, and Jabez Campbell, African Americans became involved in this Holiness movement. Smith, for example, a member of the AME Church, became acquainted with

Holiness doctrine through the preaching of Phoebe Palmer. In 1868, she received entire sanctification (the second blessing):

> Somehow I seemed to sink down out of sight of myself, and then rise; it was all in a moment. I seemed to go two ways at once, down and up. Just then such a wave came over me, and such a welling up in my heart, and these words rang through me like a bell: "God in you, God in you," and I thought doing what? Ruling every ambition and desire and bringing every thought unto captivity and obedience to His will. How I have lived through it I cannot tell, but the blessedness of the love and the peace and power I can never describe. O, what glory filled my soul! The great vacuum in my soul began to fill up; it was like a pleasant draught of cool water, and I felt it.[5]

Shortly after this experience, Smith began preaching Holiness in New York and New Jersey. Over a period of time, she developed a national reputation as an evangelist traveling to camp meetings and preaching to both whites and African Americans. Drawing on the same spiritual energy expressed by Smith and the sense of world responsibility demonstrated by the National Camp Meeting Association for the Promotion of Holiness, Levi Coppin called African Americans into the Holiness ardor and was particularly attentive to their African heritage:

> The religious field, and especially the great Continent of Africa, seems to offer the greatest opportunity for the man of color to do his work. As we stand in the open door of a new century, God is calling us to new duties and responsibilities. The preparation of this work was through a school of hard experiences, but perhaps the trials were no harder than those which have been borne by others. We waited long for the call to take our place among other agencies for the redemption of the world; and now that it has come, we have no time nor disposition to brood over\past experiences. Our business is now with the exacting present, and the portentous future, and we must adjust ourselves to the new situation.[6]

Scholars interested in the Holiness movement typically note that the first black Holiness congregations developed in the late 1800s in the rural South. One such church was the Church of the Living God founded by William Christian in Arkansas (1889). Roughly thirteen years after the first camp meeting, the Holiness passion was national in scope with spin-offs of the Holiness Association taking root on the state and local level, fueled by the preaching of hundreds of evangelists and numerous publications spreading the message.

The Holiness movement was first associated with Methodism, but this relationship became tense as the National Holiness Association grew in stature, with a sense of independence running contrary to the strict connectional and hierarchal traditions of the Methodists. This organizational conflict was heightened by the rhetoric and activity of a small group of Holiness advocates who argued the full measure of sanctification could not be achieved within any of the existing churches. Referred to as *come-outers* because of their interest in separation from existing churches in order to achieve a greater sense of holiness, these folks were uncompromising in their critique of the Methodist Church, especially focusing on their perception of the soft stance of the Methodists on worldliness (including immodest dress and secular entertainment) and its comparatively staid worship style. One must come out or remain in—there was no middle ground for Methodist ministers and laity.

Awakening event (Courtesy of Photographs and Prints Division, Schomburg Center for Research in Black Culture, The New York Public Library)

Methodists and others involved in the Great Awakenings had a concern with the possibility of freedom from sin in this life. Was it possible? How was it achieved? Radical Holiness teachings pushed beyond this basic concern by rejecting the traditional steps—gradual growth toward godliness evidenced through an increasingly pure life—preached within orthodox circles. Those embracing this position not only disagreed doctrinally with the majority, they also offended Methodists who considered themselves sanctified by excluding them and claiming sole possession of the truth. Such an assertion, and the label *saint* claimed by those in this radical Holiness movement, amounted to spiritual elitism and chauvinism. These "saints" considered themselves moving back to the original teachings of Scripture and the founders of Methodism, but Methodists regarded them as theological renegades whose claims of special status and gifts (such as healing) were unacceptable and whose style of worship lacked the order or method for which Methodism was known.

Friction between Holiness supporters and those loyal to the Methodist Church increased, resulting in efforts by the church to remove troublesome preachers who claimed a gospel that downplayed, when it did not dismiss, moves toward spiritual growth traditionally acknowledged by the church. To stem the tide of exclusionary Holiness doctrine, Methodist churches in the South passed a regulation in 1898 that gave pastors the right to refuse pulpits to Holiness evangelists. This, in effect, gave local churches the means by which to silence Holiness doctrine. Resentment from both camps—Holiness supporters and supporters of Methodism—caused many to leave the Methodist Church and start Holiness churches and denominations. Once these new churches started, they developed with a fury. By the beginning of the twentieth century, there were more than twenty Holiness denominations in existence that drew members from Methodist churches and other denominations such as the Baptist conventions.[7] Within these various churches, there was a shared sense that religious life in the United States had strayed from the scriptural ideal expressed in the Book of Acts, for example, and was in need of radical change.

Breaking with the Methodist Church did not end the controversy over Holiness. In fact, factions within the Holiness movement began giving greater attention to the manifestation of the Holy Spirit as outlined in the Book of Acts. According to the first chapter of the Acts of the Apostles, before leaving his disciples, Jesus promised they would be baptized with the Holy Spirit as with fire. In keeping with Jesus' instructions, the disciples awaited the arrival of this Spirit in

Jerusalem. "Seven weeks had gone by since Jesus' death and resurrection, and the Day of Pentecost had now arrived. As the believers met together that day, suddenly there was a sound like the roaring of a mighty windstorm in the skies above them and it filled the house where they were meeting. Then, what looked like flames or tongues of fire appeared and settled on their heads. *And everyone present was filled with the Holy Spirit and began speaking in languages they didn't know, for the Holy Spirit gave them this ability*" (italics added).[8] Some within the Holiness movement reevaluated their commitment to sanctification and the evidence of this state in light of scriptural evidence for the indwelling of the Holy Spirit. In short, they began arguing that speaking in tongues (*glossolalia*) was the scriptural sign of sanctification. They also held a strong belief, drawn from scripture, in the second coming of Christ for judgment of the earth as a real and timely event.

Interest in speaking in tongues was a step beyond the stated opinion on Holiness taught by John Wesley and held by most faithful members of the Methodist churches. Wesley argued that there was a spiritual yearning developed after salvation that required additional contact with God beyond a confession of faith. That is, salvation did not remove from the individual all signs of sin and unrighteousness. Only a "second work of grace" could remove the remaining stains of sin.[9] The difference between Wesley's theological opinion and the part of the Holiness movement that emphasized speaking in tongues was this: the new division of Holiness considered the indwelling of the Holy Spirit a *third* step, evidenced by new languages, a move beyond salvation and sanctification.[10] Christians, then, were saved by being set apart from the world for the glory of God and only then filled with the Holy Spirit and granted spiritual power and authority evidenced through speaking in tongues. To recap, the conversion experience through which an individual accepts Jesus Christ as personal Savior is followed by another act of God's grace that removes sin and brings a greater degree of righteousness. This is followed by baptism in the Holy Spirit in keeping with a strict reading of scripture, particularly the experience of the apostles in the Book of Acts. Those embracing this perspective were called Pentecostals and their movement was referred to as Pentecostalism.

Charles Fox Parham, a Kansas minister, is typically credited as being a major advocate of this doctrine concerning the baptism in the

Holy Spirit. Parham developed a theological perspective that embraced aspects of Methodism as well as Quaker doctrine. Drawing from these two traditions, he downplayed the importance of water baptism and heightened the importance of sanctification as religious development after conversion. After departing from the Methodist Church, Parham came in contact with the Fire-Baptized movement (begun in the late 1800s by Isaiah Reed and Benjamin Irwin, among others) and embraced its doctrine of the indwelling of the Holy Spirit as yet another stage of religious development coming after conversion and sanctification. With this doctrine in place, Parham began traveling as an evangelist. During his sermons, he pushed this three-stage doctrine, although he had not yet received the Holy Spirit in fulfillment of the third step. Parham eventually opened a school in Topeka, Kansas, called the College of Bethel.[11]

After scripture study, prayer, and fasting, several students at this school experienced the Holy Spirit during a worship service. Parham missed this meeting because of a preaching engagement, but upon his return he too had an experience: "Right then there came a slight twist in my throat, a glory fell over me and I began to worship God in the Swedish tongue, which later changed to other languages and continued till morning."[12] In keeping with the biblical story of the Pentecost, Parham and his students told all who would listen that they had received the Holy Spirit, evidenced by speaking in languages that they had never studied. Furthermore, the languages spoken had been recognized and confirmed by witnesses.[13] Shortly after this event, Parham closed the school and traveled around preaching salvation, regeneration, and baptism in the Holy Spirit. After spreading this Pentecostal doctrine through Kansas and Missouri, Parham settled in Houston and opened the Bible Training School in 1905.

African Americans and Pentecostalism

Among those seeking training in Pentecostal doctrine was William Seymour. Seymour was raised Baptist but migrated away from his home in Louisiana and became involved with several religious groups before coming to Holiness doctrine. In Ohio, he encountered the Evening Lights Saints Church (also known as the Church of God) and found its theology appealing. To deepen his understanding of it, Seymour took classes at the God's Bible School in Cincinnati.[14] After several years spent worshiping and studying in Ohio, Seymour moved to Houston in 1903, taking with him a strong belief in divine healing, sanctification, and the ability of God's spirit to bridge race based upon the Evening Lights Saints Church's rejection of segregation. His motivation for movement from one community to another revolved around a quest for sanctification, which he eventually came to find through the teachings of Parham. Racial prejudice and restrictions prevented Seymour from actually attending Parham's lecture, but social restrictions did not prevent him from absorbing Parham's message from the hallway. Racial discrimination and a generally lukewarm reception from Houston's church circles did not dampen Seymour's Holiness perspective. But circumstances made it fairly obvious that his ministry might be better appreciated elsewhere. Equipped with Pentecostal teachings and a desire to preach God's word, Seymour was invited in 1905 to preach at a small Holiness church named Church of the Nazarene in California. The situation, however, during his short pastorate of a church in Houston was repeated in California in that his theology (that is, the necessity of speaking in tongues) was not to the liking of the congregation. Seymour was barred from further involvement. Determined to continue his ministry, he began holding meetings in the home of Richard and Ruth Asberry on Bonnie Brae Street in Los Angeles.

An event occurred at this new location that forever changed Seymour's impact on the Pentecostal movement. During one of the Bonnie Brae Street meetings, several members of the group began speaking in tongues. A short time later, Seymour had a Pentecost experience:

> He kept on, alone, and in response to his last prayer, a sphere of white hot brilliance seemed to appear, draw near, and fall upon him. Divine love melted his heart; he sank to the floor seemingly unconscious. Words of deep healing and encouragement spoke to him. As from a great distance he heard unutterable words being uttered—was it angelic adoration and praise? Slowly he realized the indescribably lovely language belonged to him, pouring from his innermost being. A broad smile wreathed his face. At last, he arose and happily embraced those around him.[15]

Word spread and with time the gatherings were too large for the Bonnie Brae Street location. To accommodate the group, Seymour moved his services to an old building (once owned by the AME Church) at 312 Azusa Street in 1906, and he used this site as the home of a revival meeting that lasted more than three years. Eventually becoming an organized church in 1909, this revival started with a group primarily composed of women. The focus of the revival was a move back to the original church as expressed through the Pentecost experience: "The Baptism with the Holy Ghost is a gift of power on the sanctified life; so when we get it we have the same evidence as the Disciples received on the Day of Pentecost, in speaking in new tongues."[16]

William Seymour
(Courtesy of Flower Pentecostal Heritage Center)

Despite ridicule from several papers and unsympathetic religionists including Parham, Christians interested in baptism in the Holy Spirit came from diverse locations, including foreign countries. All were welcome and treated equally, and women faced few of the barriers to participation present in African American denominations. This would change with time, however, and women would find ordained ministry a difficult prospect. But during its early years, without musical instruments and devoid of any concern with time, revival services on Azusa Street were guided by Seymour but did not have a rigid order of service and did not restrict the participation of females in any way. Visitors were certain to hear testimonies, sing songs, and pray for themselves and those in need. And, of course, the major focus was speaking in tongues with the coming of the Holy

Spirit. Most scholars agree that the Pentecostal movement had wide-ranging effects. For example, in addition to a heightened sense of energetic and felt religiosity, it called for a religion that had conse-quences for daily living. In other words, Pentecostalism was con-cerned with "the relevance of religion in all of life, the nearness of the spirit world, and the interaction between and the integration of the sacred and the profane. The revolutionary desire for and expectation of the cataclysmic Second Advent of the Lord Jesus Christ to exalt the poor, the humble and the downtrodden, put down the high, the mighty and the oppressor and right every wrong. The desire and search for the spiritual power of God to accomplish in the world" what victims of society could not accomplish alone.[17]

To some extent, this theological thrust on the part of African American Pentecostalism was a critique of mainstream Methodist and Baptist churches that showed little concern for African American migrants during the Great Migration of the late nineteenth century and first several decades of the twentieth century. Many of these migrants embraced styles of worship and had socioeconomic needs that mainstream churches found difficult to deal with. But the grow-ing Pentecostal movement within African American communities, ignited by Seymour, provided opportunity for migrants to work toward a creative intersection between their religious identity and their social vision. The revival at Azusa Street caused a fire of reli-gious commitment and fervor to spread through congregations across the country. Even after the demise of the Azusa Street experience (eventually institutionalized as the Azusa Street Mission) in 1931, nine years after Seymour's death, the impact of its work continued. The largest and perhaps most widely recognized offshoot of the Azusa Street experience is the Church of God in Christ, founded by Charles Harrison Mason, which will be discussed in the next section.

◆

In summary, during the late nineteenth century many Christians were concerned with the spiritual condition of the United States. In order to bring this country into communion with God, a turn toward Holiness was initiated through revivals and camp meetings. These energetic gatherings marked the emergence of the Holiness movement. As this push toward Holiness gained momentum, divisions began to develop. For example, a radical element within the movement argued that

Holiness could not be secured within the context of existing churches because these churches were too soft on issues such as secular entertainment and immodest dress. Another conflict revolved around the indwelling of the Holy Spirit. Some believed baptism in the Holy Spirit was a third act of God's grace as evidenced by speaking in tongues. Drawing from the story in the New Testament, in which the apostles receive the Holy Spirit, advocates of speaking in tongues ignited the Pentecostal movement. The major figure in the development of Pentecostalism in African American circles is William Seymour whose three-year revival in Los Angeles brought many (blacks and whites) into the Pentecostal fold.

Study Questions

1. What sparked the Holiness movement?
2. What was the doctrinal focus of the Holiness movement?
3. How did the Holiness movement spread?
4. What is Pentecostalism?
5. What distinguishes Holiness doctrine from Pentecostalism?

The Church of God in Christ

In 1866, Charles Harrison Mason was born in Memphis, Tennessee, to former slaves. After a conversion experience in 1880 and some time on the preaching circuit, his sense of religion shifted as a result of an acquaintance with the spiritual journey of Amanda Berry Smith. Inspired by Smith, Mason made an effort to combine his new belief in sanctification with his involvement in the Baptist Church by preaching Holiness doctrine at Tabernacle Baptist Church in Alabama. His sermons pushed members of his congregation to seek a solid relationship with God through prayer, fasting, and adherence to Holiness doctrine. His ministry led to a great increase in church attendance as he pushed people to seek more than satisfaction "with the attitude merely that Holiness is right." They were to "get the experience; get saved; get a knowledge of it. Have the mind of Christ" and receive God's blessings.[18] With help from another minister, Charles P. Jones, Mason sought a larger audience for Holiness doctrine by calling for a convention after the General Association of the Baptist Church meeting in Jackson, Mississippi. In Mason's words: "At this Association, we sold our first booklet, a treatise on the twelfth chapter of I Corinthians, under the title: 'The Work of the Holy Spirit in the Churches.' We also began about this time to publish 'Truth.' Sometime after this Association, the Holy Spirit bade me call a Holiness Convention."[19] Preaching on sanctification in Mississippi as revival evangelists resulted in Mason and Jones being denied fellowship in the Baptist Association. Assisted by Jones and W. S. Pleasant, Mason held services in an old cotton gin, and steady growth led to the organization of a Holiness church, referred to as the Church of God. Founded in 1897 in Lexington, Mississippi, a revelation from God determined the church's name: Church of God in Christ (1906). This church was the first in what would quickly become a collective of like-minded congregations under the leadership of Mason and Jones. The headquarters of this new denomination was eventually moved to Memphis, Tennessee.

One year after God revealed to Mason the proper name for this church—Church of God in Christ (COGIC)—Mason convinced two others to accompany him to the Azusa Street revival. Although Mason espoused Holiness doctrine, he had not yet been baptized in the Holy Spirit himself. But hearing about the revival taking placed in Los Angeles, Mason believed it an opportunity to increase his relationship with God: "The first day of the meeting I sat by myself, away from those who went with me. I saw and heard some things that did not seem scriptural to me, but at this I did not stumble. I began to thank God in my heart for all things for when I heard some speak in tongues I knew it was right, though I did not understand it. Nevertheless it was sweet to me."[20] After some time, Mason recounts that he received the baptism of the Holy Spirit, evidenced through speaking in tongues. In his words:

It seemed that I heard the groaning of Christ on the cross dying for me. All of the work was in me until I died out of the old man. The sound stopped for a little while. My soul cried, 'Oh, God, finish your work in me.' Then the sound broke out in me again. Then I felt something raising me out of my seat without any effort of my own. I said, 'It may be imagination.' Then I looked down to see if it was really so. I saw that I was rising. Then I gave up for the Lord to have His way within me. So there came a wave of glory into me, and all of my being was

filled with the glory of the Lord. So when I had gotten myself straight
on my feet there came a light which enveloped my entire being above
the brightness of the sun. When I opened my mouth to say glory, a
flame touched my tongue which ran down to me. My language
changed and no word could I speak in my own tongue.[21]

Upon leaving Los Angeles, Mason's preaching took on Pentecostal
overtones and his revival services were marked by the manifestations
of the Holy Spirit (that is, speaking in tongues, healing, deliverance
from demons) that he had been taught to expect while in Los Angeles.[22] Taking this doctrine back to his church proved difficult. In fact,
during a meeting of the general assembly held in Memphis, Mason
requested that COGIC embrace this Pentecostal doctrine. Most
rejected this shift as did Jones, who had played a major role in the
development of the church. A schism occurred, and Jones and the
majority of the church broke away to form the Church of Christ
(Holiness), USA. Mason, meanwhile, continued as head of COGIC.
At a meeting of COGIC's general assembly held in November 1907,
Mason was made the "General Overseer and Chief Apostle" of the
twelve-member denomination. According to some accounts, COGIC
experienced rapid growth, marked by some eight hundred representatives from twenty states taking part in the denomination's tenth
anniversary meeting.[23]

Mason was convinced that the technique of sending out preachers
used during the awakenings would prove useful in the twentieth century, so his ministers went out, made converts, and formed churches.
The Great Migration provided an ample supply of displaced Christians in need of an institutional home and a religious family that
COGIC was eager to provide. Enthusiastic COGIC ministers transformed Mason's regional movement into something much more
expansive. Congregations developing in major northern cities such as
New York and Chicago were added to the strong base of support in
states such as Tennessee, Mississippi, Arkansas, Oklahoma, Texas,
and California. What resulted from this growth entailed a shift from
a primarily rural-based denomination to an urban-based one. In 1938,
COGIC had slightly better than 30,000 members in 733 churches.[24]
It would quickly grow to include over 400,000 members by the
end of the 1960s. Although primarily working class at this point, the
church's finances were impressive, allowing it to build a $400,000
temple in Memphis named the C. H. Mason Temple.

Charles H. Mason
(Courtesy of Flower Pentecostal Heritage Center)

Over the course of time, Mason also developed new positions through which he received assistance with the management of the denomination's affairs. This organizational restructuring included state overseers and bishops who worked under Mason. The role of women was also rethought during this process. Many women left Methodist and Baptist churches because of gender-based restrictions. Recognizing this potential for growth, Mason convinced Lizzie Woods Roberson to create the Women's Department within the denomination. Like the Women's Convention within the Baptist conventions, the Women's Department serves a major function with respect to both spiritual growth (including bible study and prayer bands) and material development (including an emphasis on education and other aspects of racial uplift). In addition to work through the Women's Department, many women in COGIC participate in ministry as teachers, evangelists, and in some cases chaplains. There is no doubt that African American women are a vital component of COGIC. Yet, like the other denominations discussed in this volume, women have had a difficult time securing positions of leadership in terms of ordained ministry. While recognizing their talents, COGIC stated in 1973 that the New Testament gave no strong indication that women should serve as elders, bishops, or pastors. Rather, they should play support roles through which they help men fulfill their responsibilities as church leaders.

Mason led the denomination until his death in 1961. As has been the case in most denominations managed by a charismatic figure, his death resulted in a power void that many rushed to fill. In this case, the conflict was between Ozro T. Jones and the executive board of the denomination, and it involved litigation over the course of several years. According to available records, Jones had been elected the new presiding bishop, but some raised questions concerning one person having complete authority over the denomination. Eventually, a court ruling required a constitutional convention to be held in 1968, where regulations were developed concerning the election and responsibilities of the bishop.

The organizational structure of COGIC was altered through revisions to the 1968 constitution. Accordingly, the general assembly was given control over all issues related to legislation and doctrine of the church. Those active in the general assembly include the general board, all regional bishops (who totaled more than 120, including assistant bishops who work with regional bishops), pastors and church elders, leaders of the women's division, two district missionaries, delegates from non-U.S. territories, and lay delegates. This assembly represents the highest level of authority to which church divisions (such as the council of bishops, the council of church elders, and the twelve-member general board that provides guidance for the church when the assembly is not meeting) are accountable. COGIC is similar in structure to Methodist and Baptist churches in that all three place great importance on the church's secular concerns addressed through clearly established boards and offices. For COGIC, they are the board of trustees, superintendent of property, counsel general, financial secretary, and treasurer. These positions, plus a general secretary, round out the COGIC administrative offices. There are also six denominational departments responsible for the church's efforts related to evangelism, missions, music, women, education, and the maturation of the church's young people. All of this is overseen by the presiding bishop who works with the general board.

The rethinking of leadership roles and regulations was only one consequence of the power vacuum resulting from Mason's death. A conflict over power also resulted in the formation of a splinter denomination, the Church of God in Christ, International, in 1969, which currently claims two hundred thousand members. By the time of this split, however, there were numerous Pentecostal churches throughout the United States, including First Unity of God (1927), Church of God in Christ Congregational (1932), and the Sought Out Church of God in Christ, and Spiritual House of Prayer (1947).

Noting that many Pentecostal churches had their origins within Methodist and Baptist churches, similarities are not surprising. One might think, based on the denominational structure and the strength of the presiding bishop, that COGIC resembles Methodism in its strong hierarchy and connectional authority. However, the relationship between local churches and the denomination fits more comfortably somewhere between Methodism's emphasis on central authority and the Baptist Church's sense of autonomy. On one hand, local churches must make financial contributions to the denomination similar to the assessment Methodist congregations pay annually to cover the denomination's operating costs. Yet, on the other hand, Pentecostal churches and their ministers have a degree of independence in that they can have the founder of the church as pastor for decades and this pastor can appoint a successor. This differs from the Methodist itinerant system that theoretically requires bishops to periodically move ministers to new churches, but it is similar to the practice within the Baptist conventions.

Church of God in Christ Timeline

1896 Charles Mason holds Holiness services

1896 Mason and Charles Jones form the Church of God

1897 Name of church changed to the Church of God in Christ (COGIC)

1907 Church splits with some members remaining with Mason and others firming with Jones the Church of Christ (Holiness) USA

1911 Lizzie Woods Roberson develops the Women's Department

1914 The Young People's Willing Workers Department founded

1914 White ministers leave COGIC and form the Assemblies of God

1918 Mason protests World War I

1922 Foreign missions begin

1925 Home and Foreign Mission Board developed

1939 Bishop of Foreign Fields appointed

1946 Church headquarters constructed

1961 Charles H. Mason passes away

1961 O. Thurston Jones Sr. and J. E. Bryant write the Official Manual of the COGIC

1968 Constitutional convention held

1968 New organizational structure developed

1970 J. O. Patterson established the Charles Harrison Mason Theological Seminary in Atlanta

There are, of course, distinctions between what COGIC teaches and what black Methodist and Baptist churches teach. First, all three preach the need for salvation from sin through the acceptance of Jesus Christ as one's personal Savior, followed by the attempt to live a life free of sin. But only COGIC argues that baptism of the Holy Spirit is necessary in order to have a complete and effective spiritual life. As current COGIC materials state: "the doctrine of sanctification or holiness is emphasized, as being essential to the salvation of mankind."[25] Baptists and Methodists are more likely to acknowledge various steps toward closeness to God. The Pentecostal perspective promoted by COGIC is based on a particular reading of Scripture, and Scripture is understood by its members as the infallible word of God. This depiction of Scripture is not as consistently held within Methodist and Baptist circles. Furthermore, Methodist ministers, in keeping with the *Book of Discipline*, will baptize children or adults. However, Baptists and Pentecostals reserve baptism for adults who have made a profession of faith, and baptism in this case is only by immersion. Whereas many African American Christians across denominational lines believe in the final judgment and the second coming of Jesus Christ, the uniformity of this belief is generally much stronger in the COGIC than it is in Methodist and Baptist churches. The same is true regarding other elements of doctrine such as divine healing and exorcism (or the general belief in evil spirits).

Although, in general, strong doctrinal differences remain between these various denominations, there is a growing similarity in that many churches are true to their denominational affiliation while advocating a strong interest in baptism in the Holy Spirit. Some members of these denominations refer to this as a charismatic move initiated to enliven the spiritual energy and authority of their local churches. As ministers often say, every Christian should take advantage of the gifts and tools that God makes available. Church leaders holding to this perspective remind congregations that "in the last days before the return of Jesus Christ to judge the world, God will pour out blessings and spiritual gifts on the faithful." This includes the power and spiritual authority that comes with the indwelling of the Holy Spirit.

Finally, one cannot help but wonder why all black denominations have not united as a way of centralizing their strength. Would not such a merger result in a better use of resources? The doctrinal distinctions between the various denominations are theological and ritually significant, but even these distinctions share a common connection to the struggle for religious identity and full humanity within a rather suppressive environment. There is no one way to answer the question of unification. Yet, it is important that the three major branches of black Christianity remain separate in order to preserve religious liberty and the ability to select and maintain religious affiliations that respond to particular sensibilities. This would certainly make sense in light of the religious elitism and provincialism that surfaced during the Great Migration. In this way the maintenance of a sectarian aura is in keeping with an American tradition of independence, choice, and competition. The preservation of denominational distinction also speaks to the complexity of black communities and experiences and reminds us that it is impossible to speak of religious needs in monolithic and homogeneous ways. The growth and preservation of black denominations in this sense speaks to the diversity of religious personality types.

◆

In summary, Charles H. Mason was among those making their way to Los Angeles to receive the Holy Spirit. Prior to his participation in the Azusa Street revival, Mason was a Holiness minister whose doctrine made it difficult to maintain his relationship with Baptist churches. In fact, he was denied fellowship in Baptists circles because he preached Holiness doctrine. Undeterred, Mason, with the help of several others, developed his own church, eventually named the Church of God in Christ (COGIC). Mason's contact with William Seymour's revival services changed his doctrine and created a conflict with Mason's own congregation. Those who rejected Pentecostalism left and formed the Church of God (Holiness) USA. Under Mason's leadership, COGIC, the only incorporated Pentecostal denomination until 1914, grew as ministers ordained by Mason traveled across the country creating new churches. Ministers preached a strict interpretation of the gospel that gave priority to energetic religious experience and sanctification over formalism. After Mason's death, the denomination underwent organizational restructuring but this did not hamper growth.

Selected Leaders of the Church of God in Christ

SAMUEL M. CROUCH SR. (1896–1976). Crouch began preaching as a young man and rose through the ranks to become an assistant bishop and chancellor of the Charles Harrison Mason Bible College. In addition to his positions of leadership, Crouch also served the social concerns of the church, for example, by building senior citizen housing in California while serving as pastor at Emmanuel Church of God in Christ. Crouch, however, is probably best known for being the first African American radio preacher.

OZRO THURSTON JONES SR. (1891–1972). Born in Arkansas, Jones had a conversion experience, was baptized in the Holy Spirit, and was called to preach at twenty-one years of age. Shortly after these experiences, he and his siblings began holding services in the Northwest. After two years as an evangelist, Jones took on administrative duties within the Church of God in Christ when he developed the youth department and served as its first president. His success as an administrator and preacher resulted in numerous appointments, including Pennsylvania state overseer. In 1933, Mason appointed him one of the COGIC's first bishops. Shortly after Mason's death in 1961, Jones was appointed the church's senior bishop, a position he held until 1968.

ARENIA CORNELIA MALLORY (1905–77). Although born in Illinois, Mallory spent much of her youth in Jacksonville, Florida. Because of the financial stability of her family, she was able to pursue formal education and received her master's degree from the University of Illinois. After a conversion experience, Mallory embraced the Church of God in Christ and began working as a teacher at a church school in Mississippi (Saints Junior College as of 1962). She eventually assumed leadership of the school and increased its physical plant and student body. Mallory played a major role in the National Council of Negro Women and the Holmes County Board of Education as well as several church departments such as the National Board of Education and the Women's Department.

JAMES OGLETHORPE PATTERSON SR. (1912–89). Patterson was born in Mississippi but was raised in Memphis where he studied at the Howe School of Religion in preparation for ministry. He was ordained in

1936 and served a variety of churches before building the Pentecostal Temple in Memphis. In 1953 he was made a bishop by Mason and became the presiding bishop in 1968. In this capacity, Patterson added to the church's organizational structure by building a publishing house and the church's first seminary (Charles Harrison Mason Theological Seminary). He also increased the church's financial base through the development of numerous businesses.

LIZZIE WOODS ROBERSON (1860–1945). Born in Arkansas, Roberson joined the Baptist Church in 1892. While a student at the Baptist Missionary Society School, she received the indwelling of the Holy Spirit during a service led by Mason. Roberson embraced Pentecostal doctrine and the Church of God in Christ. Shortly after joining the church, she became aware of efforts to further develop the work of women. Mason asked her to lead this effort by organizing the Women's Department. Through her leadership, women increased their involvement in a variety of the church's efforts, including missions.

Study Questions

1. What factors resulted in the formation of the Church of God in Christ?
2. What doctrine did Mason preach and how did it differ from the initial message of the Church of God in Christ?
3. What technique does the denomination use to foster church growth?
4. What structural changes occurred after Mason's death?
5. What is the church's position on women in ministry?

Suggested Reading

Patterson, J. O., et al. *History and Formative Years of the Church of God in Christ with Excerpts from the Life and Works of Its Founder, Bishop C. H. Mason.* Memphis: Church of God in Christ Publishing House, 1969. This text provides an insider's perspective on the development and mission of the Church of God in Christ (COGIC). Readers will find the attention to primary materials from the denomination's founder helpful.

Sanders, Cheryl J. *Saints in Exile: The Holiness-Pentecostal Experience in African American Religion and Culture* (New York: Oxford University Press, 1996). Sanders, a minister and professional theologian, provides information on the COGIC, which is placed in the context of the larger Holiness and Pentecostal movement. Primary examples of activities, however, are typically drawn from the COGIC. Readers will find the manner in which she discusses the theological and social development of Pentecostalism useful.

Synan, Vinson. *The Holiness-Pentecostal Tradition: Charismatic Movements in the Twentieth Century* (Grand Rapids: Eerdmans, 1971). Although Synan's perspective on black versus white roots of Pentecostalism is questionable, readers will find his discussion of Pentecostalism in the African American community helpful.

The official website of the Church of God in Christ, which includes audio recordings, is www.cogic.org/main.htm.

PART TWO

The Black Church and Social Justice

CHAPTER 4

Liberation Thought and the Black Church

What the Black Church Thinks

The institutional development and infrastructure that mark the various African American denominations provide the physical structures through which African American Christians live out their doctrines and beliefs. However, we often forget that there are links between the thought (or theology) and history (institutional structure and infrastructure) of African American denominations. In other words, the evolution of the various churches is an outgrowth of what African American Christians believed and thought. For example, Methodist denominations grew out of a theological embrace of equality and the physical ramifications of religious commitments. Is not this the meaning of Richard Allen's (the first bishop of the AME Church) actions? As historian Carol George notes, "Allen himself seemed to look at his community and denominational work as simply two different aspects of the same vocation, a view that was essential if he was to minister successfully to the comprehensive needs of his members. . . . Political considerations of one kind or another were involved in virtually all of the denomination's expansive efforts to reach unchurched members of the black community. . . ."[1]

This blending of theological reflection with current issues and denominational structure is even more clearly articulated by Baptists. Historian James Washington comments on the development of early Baptist churches: "the story of independent black Baptist congregations begins in Virginia and Georgia, where some slaves who had answered the revivalists' call for repentance during the southern phase of the revivals of the 1750s covenanted to form their own churches. They believed that spiritual bondage was a greater affliction than material bondage, and that freedom from one might lead to freedom from the other." [Beyond this] "they knew their churches were chattel arrangements. But they stubbornly trusted in the promises of the Bible that God is a liberator."[2] One also finds this direct relationship between institutional structure and theology in the development of Pentecostal churches. As scholar Iain MacRobert comments: "Black people, particularly those whose lot had not been improved by upward social mobility, were also concerned that freedom had not brought about acceptance either outside or inside the churches. Black Christian abolitionists had cried out for more than freedom. They had proclaimed that God demanded equality for black people. The twentieth-century Pentecostal movement was born at a time when fundamentalist Christians were anticipating the Second Advent and blacks were seeking a solution to the inequalities in American society."[3] Clearly, the churches discussed in this book developed and grew through a combination of thought and institutional action. In previous chapters, we have made an effort to briefly highlight key historical moments within the seven major denominations. In doing so, readers also received some information on the thought or theology undergirding the development of these churches.

The second section of this book moves us beyond an implied presentation of theology lurking behind denominational developments. To accomplish this, we give attention to one primary question: what is the theological impulse—the heart—of the Black Church implicit in the history outlined in previous chapters? This question, in turn, points us in two directions: the social gospel and black liberation theology.

◆

In summary, those who think of the Black Church as only being practice—worship and activism—fail to recognize how church activity is informed by what the church thinks. There are and have always been links between what the church does and what it says. Within all seven major denominations, African American Christians exercise their thoughts on God's will and its relationship to the world in ways that are felt.

Study Questions

1. What two elements make up the church?
2. What serves as the basis of the activism of the Black Church?

The Social Gospel

A potent approach to social transformation within churches during the 1800s and early 1900s was the social gospel (or social Christianity as it is commonly called). This activist interpretation of the Gospel of Christ first hit print and church agendas when those such as Walter Rusenchbush urged Christians to apply their faith to the elevation of poverty. Religious leaders and theologians like Rusenchbush recognized that the industrialization of the twentieth century was at best a mixed blessing in that it promoted wealth and stability, but only a small percentage of the population actually benefited from capitalism's economic boom. In essence, the cliché is correct, the "rich got richer and the poor got poorer." Although beneficial on the surface, this version of the social gospel often held a deep-seated racial chauvinism. In other words, for some social gospelers the movement of Christians in the social realm was justified by a racist sense of manifest destiny by which white Christians in the United States were recognized as God's chosen people, divinely selected to dominate the earth. This appeal to a chosen status did not first emerge with these religious teachers. Remember, for example, the rationale for the movement of pilgrims to North America. However, the twentieth century brought technological advances that increased the scope and depth of this philosophy's impact. African American ministers who were troubled by the lack of attention given to racism by white social gospelers rethought social Christianity in light of the experiences of African Americans. Although not consistently observed, this race-sensitive social Christianity was the general principle that shaped Black Church activity during Reconstruction and before. And it continued to be the operational strategy for activist preachers throughout the twentieth century.

In keeping with this call for a mirroring of Jesus' activity on behalf of the despised, a minority of preachers, including Reverdy C. Ransom of the AME Church, James Walker Hood of the AMEZ Church, Baptist minister L. K. Williams, and Adam Clayton Powell Sr., argued that the gospel called Christians to work for the betterment of African Americans by meeting a full range of needs. That is to say, spiritual development is only authentic if it pushes Christians to live the gospel's message in their everyday life. Churches with the necessary resources formalized this commitment by constructing *institutional* churches that provided job training, child care, educational opportunities, and housing as part of their religious instruction. As Reverdy Ransom put it with regard to his church in Chicago:

> The Institutional AME Church of Chicago was not born before its time. It comes to meet and serve the social conditions and industrial needs of the people, and to give answers and solutions to the many grave problems which confront our Christianity in the great centers of population of our people. It is not a dream spun out of the gossamer web of fancy; it is not an evasion, an abridgment, or a short-cut method for the realization of Christ and the Christ life in the life of the people. It is a teaching, ministering nursing-mother, and seeks through its activities and ministrations to level the inequalities and bridge the chasms between rich and poor, the educated and the ignorant, the virtuous and the vicious, the indolent and the thrifty, the vulgar and the refined, and to bring all ages and classes of the community to contribute to the common good."[4]

See also Ransom's "Duty and Destiny" in the documentary appendix. In this essay, Ransom argues that the contributions of African Americans greatly assisted in the growth of the United States and that, like all other groups, God has blessed African Americans with talents and gifts that the dominant culture should recognize, utilize, and celebrate.

Reverdy Ransom
(Courtesy of Ruth Ransom)

This was not a project undertaken by male ministers alone. Ransom's social gospel, for example, would have had little opportunity for success if not for contacts with Chicago's prominent figures through parishioner Ida B. Wells-Barnett. In addition to this role, readers will remember Wells-Barnett for her religiously inspired campaign against the lynching of African Americans.

Restrictions on ministry opportunities meant women expressed the social gospel through alternate forms of leadership. For example, as a journalist and activist, Wells-Barnett did more than most to bring mob violence, rooted in a warped desire for social control, to the attention of the American public. The need for change based upon an understanding of the Christian faith and the democratic vision are evident in her words:

> Upon the grave question presented by the slaughter of innocent men, women and children there should be an honest, courageous conference of patriotic, law-abiding citizens anxious to punish crime promptly, impartially and by due process of law, also to make life, liberty, and property secure against mob rule. Time was when lynching appeared to be sectional, but now it is national—a blight upon our nation, mocking our laws and disgracing our Christianity. "With malice toward none but with charity for all" let us undertake the work of making the "law of the land" effective and supreme upon every good of American soil—a shield to the innocent and to the guilty punishment swift and sure.[5]

The Black Church, at its best, has moved in part out of the energy and push of religious black women such as Jarena Lee, Maria Stewart, Harriet Tubman, and Sojourner Truth during the eighteenth and nineteenth centuries, and by women such as Nannie H. Burroughs, Fannie Barrier Williams, and Ida B. Wells-Barnett during the early to mid-twentieth century. But we must also remain mindful of the National Federation of Afro-American Women founded in 1895. Through this organization black women from a variety of denominations worked toward racial uplift. This organization must be understood in the context of the Women's Club movement through which African American women applied the gospel to the existential questions and concerns of the day. Considered as a whole, the work of women through various organizations and the efforts of men such as Reverdy C. Ransom, allowed the Black Church to extend itself beyond its walls. Hence, the theological claims that undergird and justify its formation are expressed through a social Christianity, which expresses an understanding of the Gospel of Christ as relevant for a world in pain.

Ida B. Wells-Barnett
(Courtesy of Library of Congress LC-USZ62-107756)

Closer to mid-twentieth century, preachers such as Adam Clayton Powell Jr. blended the best of the Christian tradition with the wisdom of the streets, a combination evident in his oft-quoted line: "Keep the faith, baby."[6] His rethinking of the church's program criticized inactivity. As Powell put it, "I am critical of those who claim to be Christian but do not carry out in their daily life this kind of religion. Next to our foreign policy no institution in our American life is more hypocritical and therefore does more to hurt the cause of God and the cause of democracy than our so-called Christian church. Next to our lack of an adequate foreign policy stands our lack of Christianity, twins of hypocrisy walking hand in hand."[7] As beneficial as these social gospelers were, they were no doubt in the minority and represented an isolated pocket of protest. Most local churches lacked the leadership, vision, and resources necessary for such multileveled ministries. Not until the Civil Rights movement did churches of varying size and stature find a method of involvement that was profoundly groundbreaking.

Growing in momentum during the 1950s and 1960s, the Civil Rights movement, through the work of figures such as Ella Baker and Fannie Lou Hamer, roused to action southern cities such as Albany, Selma, and Birmingham, while the nation watched. These activists worked for a participatory democracy through which all humans exercise a full range of life options. Much of what they understood as

the proper shape of life in the United States, as defined by this participatory democracy, stemmed from their commitment to the Christian
faith. Ella Baker gives voice to this when reflecting on her upbringing:

> Where we believed there was no sense of hierarchy, in terms of those
> who have, having a right to look down upon, or to evaluate as a lesser
> breed, those who didn't have. Part of that could have resulted, I think,
> from two factors. One was the proximity of my maternal grandparents
> to slavery. They had known what it was to not have. Plus, my grand-
> father had gone into the Baptist ministry, and that was part of the
> quote, unquote, Christian concept of sharing with others. I went to a
> school that went in for Christian training. Then, there were people
> who "stood for something," as I call it. Your relationship to human
> beings was more important than your relationship to the amount of
> money that you made.[8]

The conviction that faith in God provides the vision and motivation for work toward social transformation is also expressed by
Fannie Lou Hamer:

> We have to realize just how grave the problem is in the United States
> today, and I think the 6th chapter of Ephesians, the 11th and 12th
> verses, helps us to know how grave the problem is, and what it is we
> are up against. It says: "Put on the whole armor of God, that ye may be
> able to stand against the wiles of the devil. For we wrestle not against
> flesh and blood, but against principalities, against powers, against the
> rulers of the darkness of this world, against spiritual wickedness in
> high places." This is what I think about when I think of my own work
> in the fight for freedom, because before 1962, I would have been afraid
> to have spoken before more than six people. Since that time I have had
> to speak before thousands in the fight for freedom, and I believe that
> God gave me the strength to be able to speak in this cause.[9]

Baker, Hamer, and others were committed to the church and pushed
it to embrace the full meaning of the gospel, complete with its implications for mundane life. That is to say, being a Christian—or Christ-
like—required spirituality and a commitment to the lives of those who
suffer. In other words, "Fannie Lou Hamer placed Jesus where his
experiences, as passed through the traditions of the Black church, could
be used in the freedom struggle. She used all of this material and she
brought its full force to bear on the work she had to do."[10]

Fannie Lou Hamer
(Courtesy of Library of Congress LC-U9-12470-B)

Those who saw the pictures and news reports of unarmed black protesters attacked by police dogs, thrown around by powerful fire hoses, or beaten by police officers could not accept the conservative argument that African Americans were happy with the status quo. Nor could they believe that protestors were initiating trouble. Some might want to argue that the job of a Christian was to express love and peace—not to change the system. But this passive and inaccurate depiction of Jesus' teachings was profoundly countered by the movement and particularly Martin Luther King Jr.'s "Letter from Birmingham Jail," written in 1963. In this letter, King summarized the philosophy of the Civil Rights movement and the best of the Black Church tradition. At one point, in response to white ministers who requested that protesters wait for a more appropriate time and avoid creating conflict and allow things to be worked out slowly, King answered:

There was a time when the Church was very powerful—in the time when the early Christians rejoiced at being deemed worthy to suffer for what they believed. In those days the church was not merely a thermometer that recorded the ideas and principles of popular opinion; it was a thermostat that transformed the mores of society. . . . Things are different now. So often the contemporary Church is a weak, ineffectual voice with an uncertain sound. So often it is an arch-defender of the status quo. Far from being disturbed by the presence of the Church, the power structure of the average community is consoled by the Church's silent—and often even vocal—sanction of things as they are. But the judgment of God is upon the Church as never before. If today's Church does not recapture the sacrificial spirit of the early Church, it will lose its authenticity, forfeit the loyalty of millions, and be dismissed as an irrelevant social club with no meaning for the twentieth century.[11]

It is clear through the words of King and others mentioned above that the history and the teachings of the Black Church were not lost during the recent struggle for equality. To the contrary, the Black Church, at its best, provided the motivation and rationale for liberation activities. Both clergy and laity saw Jesus Christ as providing the example of proper conduct in order to challenge injustice in the contemporary world. In short, they were activists not in spite of their Christian faith and church membership but because this faith obligated them to fight for freedom.

Through the Civil Rights movement, the Black Church articulated theologically an attack on injustice guided by the parameters of the Christian faith. However, a faction of young activists refused to be bound by the Gospel of Christ if it did not allow them to protest in ways white America would immediately respect—to address violence with violence. Black Power advocates questioned the long-term benefits of the strategy of nonviolent action, especially in the face of the violence of beatings, water hoses, police dogs, bombings, and general abuse met by blacks during protest activities. This friction between the highly Christian emphasis of the majority within the Civil Rights movement and the growing social critique by Black Power advocates who did not necessarily hold to Christian doctrine climaxed with the assassination of Martin Luther King Jr. in 1968.

◆

In summary, the social gospel encouraged Christians to put their faith to work on behalf of the physical, everyday needs of African Americans, particularly those problems resulting from the Great Migration. While some neglected the physical needs of migrants, preferring to preach personal salvation, a small number of churches worked to

Social Gospel and Civil Rights Movement Timeline

1955 (DEC. 1)	Rosa Parks arrested, sparking the Montgomery Bus Boycott
1955 (DEC. 5)	Martin Luther King Jr. elected head of the MIA (Montgomery Improvement Association)
1956 (NOV. 13)	U.S. Supreme Court rules against bus segregation
1956 (DEC. 21)	Montgomery Bus Boycott ends
1957 (FEB. 14)	King becomes head of Southern Christian Leadership Conference (SCLC)
1961 (DEC. 15)	Albany, Georgia: Albany movement to end segregation gains assistance from King
1961 (AUG. 10)	Demonstrations in Albany end
1963 (APR. 3)	Protest campaign in Birmingham
1963 (APR. 16)	King writes "Letter from Birmingham Jail"
1963 (MAY 10)	Settlement reached to desegregate facilities such as lunch counters and to increase job opportunities for blacks
1963 (JUNE 11)	Kennedy announces Civil Rights plans
1963 (JUNE 12)	Medgar Evers assassinated
1963 (AUG. 28)	King addresses the March on Washington
1963 (SEPT. 15)	Four young girls killed in church bombing
1963 (NOV. 22)	John F. Kennedy assassinated
1964 (FEB. 9)	Protest in St. Augustine, Florida, begins
1964 (MAR. 12)	Malcolm X leaves the Nation of Islam
1964 (JULY 2)	Civil Rights Act signed
1964 (JULY 21)	"Freedom Summer" campaign in Mississippi
1965 (FEB. 1)	Struggle in Selma
1965 (FEB. 21)	Malcolm X assassinated
1965 (JULY 26)	Chicago Campaign begins
1965 (AUG. 11–15)	Watts Rebellion
1966 (JUNE 16)	Black Power Slogan
1966 (AUG. 12)	King criticizes Vietnam war
1967 (DEC. 4)	Poor People's campaign
1968 (APR. 4)	King assassinated

continue the tradition of racial uplift through job training programs, housing, educational opportunities, and child care. This emphasis on social Christianity hit a high point during the Civil Rights movement when churches provided the meeting space, resources, and bodies necessary to undertake nonviolent direct action.

Selected Social Gospel and Civil Rights Leaders

FANNIE LOU HAMER (1917–77). Hamer was born in Mississippi and spent her early years working with her parents, who were cotton share-croppers. The need for her to contribute to the family's finances made it impossible for Hamer to continue her education beyond rudimentary reading and writing. Instead of school, she spent her time weighing cotton. However, as the Civil Rights movement got underway, she volunteered to help African Americans register to vote. Hamer quickly became known for her organizing work and speeches concerning civil rights activities in Mississippi. Hamer also played a major role in the formation of the Mississippi Freedom Democratic Party.

JAMES WALKER HOOD (1831–1918). Hood was born in Pennsylvania to tenant farmers. Financial limitations and frequent moves kept him from receiving a formal education, but this did not prevent him from succeeding as a minister in the African Methodist Episcopal Zion Church. Licensed to preach in 1856 and ordained in 1860, Hood left to serve as a missionary in Nova Scotia. This assignment was followed by missionary work in North Carolina where Hood was largely responsible for the church's growth in that area of the South. In 1872, Hood was elected a bishop and continued his work in North Carolina where he played a major role in the founding of Livingstone College and several of the church's journals. Throughout his years of ministry, Hood demonstrated a concern with both the spiritual and physical needs of African Americans that mirrors the best of the social gospel tradition.

MARTIN LUTHER KING JR. (1929–68). King was born into a prominent Baptist family in Atlanta and attended Morehouse College. After expressing an interest in ministry, King attended Crozier Theological Seminary and Boston University where he received his Ph.D. But prior to completing his education, he accepted the pastorate of Dexter Baptist Church in Montgomery, Alabama. There King became involved in the Montgomery Bus Boycott that ultimately evolved into the Civil Rights movement. The success of the boycott increased his stature and led to his election as president of the Southern Christian Leadership Conference. He moved to Atlanta to head this organization and co-pastor at his father's Ebenezer Baptist Church. Over the next several years, King drew from the Black Church tradition and the philosophy of Mahatma Gandhi to develop a nonviolent direct action method of protest that forever changed race relations in the United States.

Martin Luther King Jr.
(Courtesy of Library of Congress LC-U9-11696)

ADAM CLAYTON POWELL JR. (1908–72). Powell, whose father was the influential pastor of Abyssinian Baptist Church in New York, was educated at Colgate University and Union Theological Seminary. After his father retired, Powell became pastor of Abyssinian where he developed a unique version of the social gospel. After leading successful protest in Harlem for jobs and other opportunities for African Americans, Powell entered politics. In 1941, he was elected to the New York Council and three years later he was elected to the United States Congress. In Washington, Powell sponsored numerous pieces of legislature concerned with job and educational opportunities for the poor. After years of conflict between Powell and Congress, he lost his congressional seat to Charles Rangel.

IDA B. WELLS-BARNETT (1862–1931). Although born prior to the emancipation of the slaves, Wells-Barnett received a formal education from Rust College and became a journalist and activist. She is probably best known for her work against the lynching of African Americans. Her writings on the subject stirred a great deal of hostility in the South, but Wells-Barnett continued her efforts. Developing a national and international reputation based upon her anti-lynching campaign, she played a major role in exposing the deep strains of racism within the country. She also played a major role in the struggle for full rights for women.

Study Questions

1. What is the social gospel?
2. What was the impact of the social gospel on Black Church ministry?
3. What role did women play in the social gospel movement?
4. What is the relationship between the social gospel and the Civil Rights movement?
5. Who were some of the social gospel's major advocates?

Suggested Reading

Crawford, Vicki L., Jacqueline Anne Rouse, and Barbara Woods, eds. *Women in the Civil Rights Movement: Trailblazers and Torchbearers, 1941–1965.* Brooklyn, N.Y.: Carlson, 1990. This book breaks any assumptions that the Civil Rights movement was a male movement. In so doing, it provides a glimpse into the social gospel from the perspective of African American women.

Harding, Vincent. *Hope and History: Why We Must Share the Story of the Movement.* Maryknoll, N.Y.: Orbis, 1990. This history of the rationale and purpose of the Civil Rights movement benefits from the author's firsthand experience of the movement.

Hine, Darlene Clark, Wilma King, and Linda Reed, eds. *"We Specialize in the Wholly Impossible": A Reader in Black Women's History.* Brooklyn, N.Y.: Carlson, 1995. Like the Crawford text, this volume provides important information on the role of women in social transformation activities, but with a much wider historical scope beyond the Civil Rights movement.

Luker, Ralph E. *The Social Gospel in Black and White: American Racial Reform, 1885–1912.* Chapel Hill: University of North Carolina Press, 1991. Luker provides an important study of the social gospel within African American circles and places this within the larger movement, including its often expressed insensitivity to issues of race.

Paris, Peter J. *Black Leaders in Conflict: Joseph H. Jackson, Martin Luther King, Jr., Malcolm X, Adam Clayton Powell, Jr.* New York: Pilgrim, 1978. Paris provides a critical and comparative study of major religious leaders of the twentieth century.

The following site provides information and links to other sites that allow readers to explore both the historical and contemporary activism of the Black Church: www.BlackandChristian.com.

Black Liberation Theology

For many, the assassination of Martin Luther King Jr. was a turning point. Those who had committed themselves to the ethic of love and the social vision of Christianity as the proper framework for the Civil Rights movement were faced with a dilemma: Did the murder of King and its ramifications point to the inadequacy of the Christian faith for social transformation? Some answered yes, but many more refused to completely reject Christianity and its theology. Those maintaining a commitment to the Christian faith, however, could not ignore the radical social critique by the Black Power movement. Emerging in the late 1960s, this movement gave more allegiance to the social vision of Malcolm X than to King's. Not wanting to dismiss either perspective, some within the Black Church sought to reconcile the two by radicalizing Christian faith.

This effort to bridge the gap between the Black Church and Black Power actually predates King's assassination. In fact, an earlier sign of this effort was the 1966 ad hoc committee formed by Benjamin Payton of the National Council of Churches and a host of ministers representing various denominations. This group, called the National Committee of Negro Churchmen (NCNC), attempted to interpret Black Power in light of the Christian gospel. On July 31, 1966, one year after the assassination of Malcolm X, the NCNC printed a statement of purpose in the *New York Times*: "Our purpose here is neither to beg nor to borrow, but to state the determination of black men in America to exact from this nation not one whit less than our full manhood rights. We will not be cowed nor intimidated in the land of our birth. We intend that the truth of this country, as experienced by black men, will be heard. We shall state this truth from the perspective of the Christian faith and in the light of our experience with the Lord of us all, in the bleakness of this racially idolatrous land."[12] It would take more than a decade for this growing theological perspective to recognize the problems inherent in its sexist language and assumptions, but at this point the major concern was the demonic racism destroying black America.

In the 1966 statement, the NCNC addressed four groups: national leaders, white churchmen, black citizens, and the mass media. In each case an appeal was made for a rethinking of power dynamics that bred pain and suffering within African American communities. This

Malcolm X
(Courtesy of Library of Congress LC-U9-11696)

entailed an understanding of the riots and other events of the 1960s as a minor threat to national security. The major threat was seen as the nation's failure to live in accordance with God's demand for justice and righteousness. This move into the full expression of God's will cannot be achieved through rhetorical commitments to love (which is simply acceptance of the status quo) and appeals to U.S. individualism over against community (that is, a healthy self-concept in the context of group dynamics—humanity). The NCNC states:

> The fundamental distortion facing us in the controversy about 'Black Power' is rooted in a gross imbalance of power and conscience between Negroes and white Americans. It is this distortion, mainly, which is responsible for the widespread, though often inarticulate, assumption that white people are justified in getting what they want through the use of power, but that Negro Americans must, either by nature or by circumstance, make their appeal only through conscience. As a result, the power of white men and the conscience of black men have both been corrupted.[13]

Power, therefore, must be secured in order to more fully participate in the important processes of the nation.[14]

This was the first statement on Black Power issued by members of the Black Church and its impact was far reaching. More than just a theological justification for Black Power, its philosophical rationale was a commitment by black churches to the welfare of African Americans using new tools of changing times, even if its overall tone is mild by today's standards. Most black churches, however, gave scant attention to this document and its implications. But being ignored by denominational leaders did not stop the NCNC from institutionalizing itself through the development of a headquarters in Harlem as well as a national center in Dallas.

Members of this committee realized that the 1966 statement necessitated continued work on theology within the context of black life. In 1967, during its first national convocation, a subgroup was given responsibility for explicating the basic rubrics of such a theology. It was clear that it had to be a religiously based description of Black Power true to the liberative connotation of the gospel articulated by King but without being bound to the *suffering servant* implications of King's theology. This statement sparked a great deal of conversation—both pro and con—and was followed by other declarations, including the extremely controversial "Black Manifesto" prepared in the context of the National Black Economic Development Conference in Detroit (April 26, 1969) and read by James Forman at Riverside Church in New York City. The manifesto critiqued the historically documented oppressive behavior of Europeans and called upon African Americans to recognize themselves as connected to Africa. Furthermore, it called for African American control over economic development as a way of ending exploitation by "racist white America," a country that has raped "our minds, our bodies, our labor" for centuries. But in order to construct economic opportunity and self-sufficiency for African Americans, the manifesto called white Christians and Jews to provide financial resources (reparations) because these groups had aided in the exploitation of people of color across the globe.[15]

This statement could not be ignored, particularly by concerned black clergy who were wrestling with the relevance of the Christian gospel in a context of modern racism. The board of directors of the National Committee of Black Churchmen (NCBC, formerly the NCNC) responded to the manifesto and to the growing unrest in major urban areas with an embrace of Black Power in light of the teachings of Jesus Christ (that is, Christian conscience). In essence, the NCBC affirmed the critique of American culture raised in the manifesto and supported the call for financial compensation, from religious organizations *and* private foundations, for the centuries of free labor.[16]

This positive response to the manifesto was followed by numerous other documents, including a 1969 statement of the basic tenets of black theology (included in the documentary appendix following this chapter). Black theology, according to NCBC, is an articulation of a commitment to freedom in the context of the United States first expressed in the spirituals and the workings of the early Black Church. In a word, "All theologies arise out of communal experience with God. At this moment in time, the black community seeks to express its theology in language that speaks to the contemporary mood of black people." Black theology of liberation was more precisely defined in the following way: "The word 'Black' in the phrase was defined by the life and teachings of Malcolm X—culturally and politically embodied in the Black Power movement. The term 'theology' was influenced by the life and teachings of Martin Luther King, Jr.—religiously and politically embodied in the Black Church and the Civil Rights movement. The word liberation was derived from the past and contemporary struggles for political freedom and the biblical story of the Exodus, as defined by the Black religious experience in the United States."[17]

Numerous figures, including C. Eric Lincoln, Vincent Harding, and Albert Cleage, participated in the preparation of these documents and, hence, in the early formation of a black liberation theology. However, as an academic discipline of inquiry, most acknowledge that the basic framework emerged in the writings of James H. Cone. In his intellectual autobiography, Cone argues that as a Christian committed to the freeing of African Americans from oppression he was, in essence, locked in a struggle to bring the Christian gospel in line with the radical social critique offered by Malcolm X. His was an effort to recover the liberative nature of the Christian gospel—the revolutionary actions of Christ—that had been covered by centuries of Christian complacency. For Cone, to do so required great attention to numerous overlooked theological resources, such as African American history, African American cultural production, and African American experience, as well as scripture and the Christian tradition. These resources were viewed with an eye on the duplicity of European renderings of history and faith, as well as a primary focus on the welfare of African Americans. In Cone's words:

> Because a perspective refers to the whole of a person's being in the context of a community, the sources and norm of black theology must be consistent with the perspective of the black community. Inasmuch as white American theologians do not belong to the black community, they cannot relate the gospel to that community. Invariably, when white theology attempts to speak to blacks about Jesus Christ, the gospel is presented in the light of the social, political, and economic interests of the white majority. (One example of this is the interpretation of Christian love as nonviolence.) Black theologians must work to destroy the corruptive influence of white thought by building theology on sources and a norm that are appropriate to the black community.[18]

This methodology marked a radical break from traditional forms of theological discourse in that it gave preference to the lived experience of African Americans instead of the experiences of whites. In other words, it did not allow white Americans to view their experience as the measure for all people. It did not allow white Americans to think of their self-interest as the priority for all people. On the contrary, it demanded that African Americans speak about their own needs and self-interest in light of their unique experiences. Furthermore, it was an assertion of the relevance of the Black Church in the struggle for a liberated existence.[19] His assertions entailed a commitment to Christ as a radical, black Messiah who, in keeping with the will of God, was concerned with the disruption of institutions and mind-sets that only reinforced the status quo. In fact, his goal was to "identify liberation as the heart of the Christian gospel and blackness as the primary mode of God's presence."[20]

Although the above perspective was radical enough in the late 1960s, perhaps the most challenging component of Cone's theology revolved around the idea of God as ontologically black. That is to say, God is so strongly identified with the oppressed—best understood in the United States with respect to African Americans—that God's being (or identity) becomes synonymous with this group. By extension, commitment to God's will as expressed in the Christian faith requires the same sort of strong commitment to the oppressed from all Christians. In short, in the context of the United States, true Christians must become ontologically black. For the church-based theologians articulating this vision, true Christian conduct had to entail attention to the liberation of oppressed communities and reconciliation between communities. This should be based on respect, appreciation, and a biblically inspired recognition of all humanity's creation in the image of God. We end this discussion with an extended quotation from Cone on the subject of God as black.

> Because blacks have come to know themselves as *black*, and because that blackness is the cause of their own love of themselves and hatred of whiteness; the blackness of God is the key to our knowledge of God. The blackness of God, and everything implied by it in a racist society, is the heart of the black theology doctrine of God. There is no place in black theology for a colorless God in a society where human beings suffer precisely because of their color. The black theologians must reject any conception of God which stifles black self-determination by picturing God as a God of all peoples. Either god is identified with the oppressed to the point that their experience becomes God's experience, or god is a God of racism. . . . Because God has made the goal of blacks' God's own goal, black theology believes that it is not only appropriate but necessary to begin the doctrine of God with an insistence on God's blackness. The blackness of God means that God has made the oppressed condition God's own condition.[21]

Black Theology within the Church

Although most scholars writing black theology claim a connection to the Black Church, it must be acknowledged that most black churches have given little explicit attention to the development of this academic theology. According to minister and theologian James H. Harris:

> Few ministers and laypersons who labor in black churches are aware that black theology is a discipline of study and reflection. Consequently, interest in and understanding of black liberation theology barely exists among the majority of persons that I have encountered in the black church. . . . many black pastors still think that black academicians who construct theology outside of the practices of the church are largely out of touch with the very people about whom they claim to write. Because of this perception, few black ministers read and teach the works of prominent black theologians. . . . Even fewer laypersons are familiar with the tenets of black liberation theology.[22]

This is the perception, but is the gap as large as some believe and is it an unavoidable necessity? A suspicion exists about professional black theologians and academics in general that their expertise in abstract thought has come at the expense of an appreciation of the lived experience of African Americans. We believe this suspicion is often intensified with respect to the church, where many are still told not to "go to school and lose Jesus." There is no doubt that some have gone off to college and graduate school and for various reasons have moved away from the church. But there is no reason to believe this is the case for all, especially those theologians who publicly claim a love for and connection to the Black Church. According to historian Gayraud Wilmore, it is this connection to the church that separated black theology in its early years from secular black nationalism. That is, "the traditional orientation of the church to the gifts and demands of the gospel of love, its inclination to bring everything that concerns

---

Black Theology Timeline

1966   National Council of Churches forms ad hoc committee (National Committee of Negro Churchmen) to address Black Power in light of the Christian gospel

1966   NCNC publishes a full-page piece in the *New York Times* outlining its thoughts on Black Power

1966   NCNC publishes a piece in the *New York Times* dealing with issues of race and economics

1967   NCNC holds first national conference on Black Power

1967   NCNC holds first national conference on urban problems in response to riots in several cities

1967   NCNC changed to the National Committee of Black Churchmen

1968   NCBC issues statement on the "Urban Mission in a Time of Crisis"

1969   Black Manifesto written during the Black Economic Development Conference

1969   James Forman reads the Black Manifesto at Riverside Church (New York)

1969   NCBC begins dialogue with African theologians

1969   NCBC issues statement on black theology

1969   James Cone publishes *Black Theology and Black Power*

1970   NCBC publishes "The Black Declaration of Independence" in the *New York Times*

1970   Society for the Study of Black Religion founded in order to bring scholars of black religion into conversation

1970   Cone publishes *A Black Theology of Liberation*, the first systematic presentation of black theology

it 'under the feet of Christ,' and its penchant for reconciliation rather than protracted enmity, provided Black theology with a certain attitude and language that qualified its secularity and differentiated it from the reckless and belligerent ideology and rhetoric of Black Power revolutionaries like H. Rap Brown, Eldridge Cleaver, and James Forman."[23]

The creators and current spokespersons of black theology argue that it is merely an extension of the Black Church's historically defined thought and commitments. We believe there is something to be said for this argument. That is, even the short discussion of Black Church history and thought presented here demonstrates links—some subtle and others pronounced—between the words and efforts of black theology and the words and efforts of the Black Church over the course of its existence. Put another way, most black theologians consider themselves to be translating the history and activism of the Black Church into the language of theology. They share a common mission, although the language and frameworks used to express it may be different. This, however, need not create a deep difference between the two. Dwight Hopkins, a theologian at the University of Chicago, points to the challenges that professional theologians face in maintaining links to the lived community of faith:

> The second generation of Black theologians [those trained after 1970] faces the challenge of preserving positive and critical ties to the Black Church and other intimate faith organizations. The church is one community that holds us accountable to the liberation faith mandate in the gospel and African-American tradition. The church also helps to nurture our growth. But most of the educational system in the United States, particularly for full-time professors, pulls us away from meaningful organized faith communities. The academy seeks to perpetuate itself. And like all groups, it has established methods to suck professors into its own world. In this world, advancement and staying power depend on how well we give all of our time to publishing, teaching, and serving the academy. Clearly part of the gap between Black professors and the pew results from a well-organized educational system that demands our time. Still, we must maintain creative and critical relationships to the Black church. . . . [24]

What Hopkins and others are expressing is a recognition of the ways in which life as an academic can separate theologians from the day-to-day realities of the Black Church and the black community.

This is the recognition of a challenge—not an unbridgeable gulf. Black theologians want to believe that creative avenues for conversation between themselves and the churches to which they claim allegiance will point out the many areas of agreement and the ability for sustained conversation and partnership.

While this creative engagement will point out areas of connection, it will also point out areas of disagreement. Black theology has in some ways extended or challenged the mission of the Black Church, and this has also made it difficult for black theology to find a ready audience in many churches, particularly more theologically conservative churches. The more liberal stance on sexuality, for example, expressed by many theologians has certainly been a point of contention. One can understand this, however, as the obligation of the theologian to both praise the church for what it does well and to push or challenge the church to rethink its stance or work in other areas. This is a give-and-take as old as the church itself. For example, Jarena Lee and Julia Foote, although not professional theologians, pushed the church to rethink its stance on women in ministry, which ultimately benefited the church. Reverdy C. Ransom and James W. Hood urged the church to rethink its obligations to black migrants, which also benefited the church. Although she was not a member of one of the denominations mentioned here, Pauli Murray also challenged the Christian church to recognize its racism as well as push black theologians to acknowledge their sexism, which is clearly evident in the language of their writings (see the documentary appendix). In so doing Murray lays the academic groundwork for Womanist theology of liberation developed in the late 1970s and early 1980s through the writings of Jacquelyn Grant, Katie Cannon, and Delores Williams.

While Grant, Cannon, and Williams provide a more systematic presentation of liberation theology from the perspective of Black women, Frances Beale joins Murray in providing an early rationale for later writings on sexism in the church. In an article published in 1970 called "Double Jeopardy: To Be Black and Female," she highlights the manner in which African American women's experience is defined by racism and sexism and argues that this reality means "those who are exerting their 'manhood' by telling Black women to step back into a domestic, submissive role are assuming a counter-revolutionary position."[25] Beale calls for a reevaluation of the meaning of liberation in order to include the concerns and needs of African American women (who represent the majority population within African American communities) as part of the blueprint for social transformation. In order to contextualize this call, Beale outlines the various forms of manipulation and oppression African American women have historically faced. She concludes the essay with a suggestion:

> Given the mutual commitment of Black men and Black women alike to the liberation of our people and other oppressed peoples around the world, the total involvement of each individual is necessary. A revolutionary has the responsibility not only of toppling those that are now in a position of power, but of creating new institutions that will eliminate all forms of oppression. We must begin to rewrite our understanding of traditional personal relationships between man and woman. All the resources that the Black community can muster up must be channeled into the struggle. Black women must take an active part in bringing about the kind of society where our children, our loved ones, and each citizen can grow up and live as decent human beings, free from the pressures of racism and capitalist exploitation.[26]

As church leaders from the eighteenth century to the late twentieth century have demonstrated, there has always been a need within the Black Church for self-critique and correction because this is the way individuals and groups improve and grow. Therefore, when Black theologians provide a critique of certain church policies and practices, it is not a matter of separation from the church or dislike for the church. Rather, for those who speak about a personal relationship with the church, it is a matter of pushing the church to be better, to do more, and to mean more to those who suffer. As Cone notes, there are some who understand black theology as "the prophetic voice of the black church, calling it back to its liberating heritage, thereby enabling it to become a more effective instrument of black liberation."[27] A concern with quality of life, liberty, and freedom as an outgrowth of devotion to God is basic to both the Black Church and black theology.

Black Theology outside the Church

It is true that black theology has made a conscious effort to connect itself to the Black Church. In some cases this has been successful, but in many cases the effectiveness and depth of this connection remain an open question. Most have assumed this connection is a necessity, but is it? That is, must all black theology be connected to the church? Whereas there have been undeniable benefits derived from efforts to forge this link, it has also resulted in a common understanding that the legitimacy of black theology is determined by a connection to the church—it is not black theology unless it is connected to the Black Church. This is problematic because it has the potential to exclude theologians with less direct links to the church. Some, falsely we believe, argue that those who are without direct links to the church are not really doing theology. Addressing this problem is simple: There needs to be a general recognition of various black theologies, not only those that are connected to the Black Church.

More important for the purposes of this book and less easily addressed is the manner in which a mandatory connection between theology and the church can result in black theologians compromising their critique of certain Black Church actions for fear of losing their links to the church. We have no solution to this dilemma, and some may not consider it a dilemma at all. We simply suggest that the relationship between some forms of black theology and the Black Church be acknowledged and given thoughtful consideration, recognizing the benefits of this engagement while also being sensitive to its possible liabilities or limitations.

◆

In summary, in 1966 the National Committee of Negro Churchmen (NCNC) was formed as a response to the Black Power movement. Through printed materials and conferences it worked to bring the Christian gospel and Black Power in line. In so doing, the NCNC argued that the basic premise of the gospel is the liberation of the oppressed; hence, both the gospel and Black Power are concerned with the welfare of those who suffer at the hands of the powerful. Ministers and academics who took this proposition seriously began developing a form of theology sensitive to the experiences of African Americans. This black theology called all Christians to join in the struggle for social transformation through the destruction of power structures that run contrary to the call of Jesus Christ for justice and equality.

Selected Leaders in Black Theology

Jaramogi Abebe Agyeman (Albert B. Cleage Jr.) (1911–2000). Agyeman (Cleage) was born in Indiana. He attended Wayne State University and Oberlin School of Theology before being ordained in the Congregational Church. He served as pastor of numerous churches before his growing sense of black nationalism and emerging black theology forced his break with traditional Congregational Church structure. He founded the Shrine of the Black Madonna as a revolutionary religious organization committed to the communal salvation of African Americans and, in 1972, all links with the Congregational denomination were rejected through the formation of the Pan African Orthodox Christian Church. From this church, he played a role in the developing debate over black power and Christian faith. His 1968 book, *The Black Messiah*, pushed those involved in the growing black theology program to think beyond the "soft" turn-the-other-cheek theology espoused by King. Within this and subsequent writings, he argued for a Christian nationalism premised upon devotion to a black God and the black revolutionary redeemer, Jesus Christ. His doctrine of God and Jesus Christ appear to have influenced the writings of James Cone and other Black theologians.

James Hal Cone (1938–). Cone was born in Arkansas and educated at Philander Smith College, Garrett Theological Seminary, and Northwestern University, where he earned a Ph.D. in 1965. He is an ordained minister within the African Methodist Episcopal Church. Cone currently teaches at Union Theological Seminary in New York and is responsible for training many of those involved in black theology. He is recognized as a major architect in the formation of black theology through his numerous publications. In fact, his *Black Theology and Black Power* (1969) and *A Black Theology of Liberation* (1970) represent the first two academic books on black theology.

Pauli Murray (1910–1986). Murray was born in Baltimore. She received her B.A. from Hunter College. After working for several years, Murray applied for graduate work at the University of North Carolina but was denied admission because of race. This brush with racism in the South sparked her interest in legal studies as a way of reshaping race relations in the United States and led to her studying law at Howard University. After graduating, Murray studied for the LL.M. at Boalt Hall of Law (University of California, Berkeley). With these degrees in hand, Murray held several important positions, including being the first black deputy attorney general in California and the first female attorney at a major law firm in New York. Murray published and taught until the death of a friend sparked a desire to enter ministry. After receiving her M.Div. from General Theological Seminary in 1977, Murray was ordained the first female African American Episcopal priest. Murray's ministry and writings were marked by a concern with the gospel's impact on liberation efforts. Her theological writings are among the earliest critiques of the sexism within black theology and the racism within feminist theology.

J. DEOTIS ROBERTS (1927–). Roberts was born in North Carolina and educated at Shaw University, Hartford Theological Seminary, and Edinburgh University in Scotland. An ordained Baptist minister, Roberts held several ministerial posts but is best known for his work as a professor and administrator at several institutions including Howard University Divinity School, the Interdenominational Theological Center, and Eastern Baptist Theological Seminary. Roberts was a major voice in the development of black theology, challenging his colleagues to think about liberation and reconciliation as simultaneous processes. He presented this in book form with the publication of his first in a series of texts, *Liberation and Reconciliation: A Black Theology* (1971). Roberts was a member of the NCBC and remains an active participant in the ongoing development of black theology.

GAYRAUD S. WILMORE JR. (1921–). Wilmore was born in Philadelphia. After serving in the military, he prepared for ministry in the Presbyterian Church through study at Lincoln University, Lincoln University Theological Seminary, and, some years later, Temple University. Over the course of approximately a decade, Wilmore worked with the Student Christian movement and the United Presbyterian Church Board of Christian Education. He also played a major role in the founding of the NCBC and the Society for the Study of Black Religion. In 1960, he accepted a teaching post at Pittsburgh Theological Seminary and has taught at several institutions since then. His book,

Black Religion and Black Radicalism, first published in 1970, was a groundbreaking discussion of the Black Church's less than consistent participation in the liberation struggle.

Study Questions

1. What was the purpose of the NCNC?
2. How was Black Power described by the NCNC?
3. What is black theology?
4. How would you describe the relationship between professional theologians and the Black Church?
5. In what ways can black theology be developed inside and outside of the church?

Suggested Reading

Cone, James H. *A Black Theology of Liberation*. Maryknoll, N.Y.: Orbis, 1989. This is the first systematic treatment of black theology. It provides the basic framework that influenced all subsequent formations of liberation theology in the African American context.

Cone, James H. and Gayraud Wilmore, eds. *Black Theology: A Documentary History, 1966–1979*. Maryknoll, N.Y.: Orbis, 1969. This provides the best collection of primary documents related to the development and critique of black theology during its early years.

Roberts, J. Deotis. *Liberation and Reconciliation: A Black Theology*. Philadelphia: Westminster, 1973. In this book, Roberts argues that black theology is misguided unless it recognizes that liberation and reconciliation must be sought simultaneously.

Skinner, Tom. *How Black Is the Gospel?* Philadelphia: Lippincott, 1970. This book provides a black theology discussion of the Gospel of Christ as a gospel of liberation and social transformation.

Thurman, Howard. *Jesus and the Disinherited*. Nashville: Abingdon-Cokesbury, 1949. Thurman provides an interesting pre-black theology discussion of the social implications of Jesus' ministry.

Washington, Joseph R. *The Politics of God*. Boston: Beacon, 1967. After writing an earlier critique of the Black Church that received a great deal of negative attention, Washington modifies his perspective in this book. Here he argues that black religion may be the source of transformation in the United States because white churches have become more interested in economics and the status quo than in freedom.

The website of the Congress of National Black Churches is www.cnbc.org. The CNBC is a collective of Black denominations concerned with community outreach.

The official website for the Leadership Center (at Morehouse College) developed by Walter Fluker is www.morehouse.edu/leadership center/index.htm. One of the programs administered by the center concerns the public work of black churches.

The following two documents are provided in order to give readers samples of the two forms of liberation thought outlined in chapter four. Readers interested in a more detailed and extensive presentation of documents related to liberation thought in the Black Church will find the suggested reading lists in chapter 4 helpful.

Social Gospel

Reverdy C. Ransom, "Duty and Destiny," in the *AME Church Review*, April 1905, 316–22.

In this piece, Ransom wrestles with fundamental issues related to the situation of African Americans in the United States. Much of this borders on notions of manifest destiny and the way in which each human group contributes something unique to civilization and culture. Notions of manifest destiny popular during Ransom's time marked the Anglo-Saxon as God's chosen and justified in "subduing" both land and other humans. Ransom's effort, in this piece and elsewhere, is to counter this argument through the language of duty to God and humanity—collective destiny—democracy and justice.

◆

How strangely, indeed, are we begirth in the midst of this mighty current of humanity of which we form so small a part. How did I become what I am? How was I fashioned thus, in thought, character and in circumstance? Did I become what I am because of what I was? Does what I shall become depend unalterably upon what I am? What of those paths that lead one to poverty, another to wealth; one to fame, another to oblivion; one to political subjugation, another to political control?

Is individual or national destiny a part of a fixed order in the scheme of things? Or, is destiny something to be attained, achieved; something under the influence and guidance of capacity, courage, character? I doubt not that each individual, as well as nation, has felt within him at least a dim foreshadowing of his destiny. A race conceives that destiny has decreed it to be superior and therefore it has a right to hold and treat all others as inferior; a nation feels that destiny has given it the sceptre of empire and therefore it has the right to subjugate and govern, without their consent certain peoples; the individual feels that destiny has decreed him enjoyment of certain rights in human society, and therefore to achieve his destiny he is justified in fighting for his rights.

Jesus Christ, in dealing with the great question of human destiny, speaks not once of human rights. He does not teach men how to obtain their rights, but how to fulfill their duties. He teaches that the loftiest exercise of our faculties and powers lies in the fulfillment of our duty toward God and man. Joseph Mazzini, the great Italian patriot, wisely based his teaching and philosophy upon this doctrine, that rights could only be attained by the fulfillment of duties. I should refuse to be a slave, because it is my duty to be free; I should refuse to be kept in ignorance because it is my duty to be enlightened; I should refuse to be under tyranny of another man, because it is my duty to be also a man. It becomes thus, then, a greater thing to fulfill a duty than it is to assert a right.

We have heard much of the man of destiny in ancient times, and even in modern times he is thought to have occasionally appeared. Was it the star of destiny that led the invincible legions of Julius Caesar back to Rome; or was it not rather that Brutus, the envious Casca, and Cassius, " with the lean and hungry look, who thought too much", were eclipsed in oratory, literature, statesmanship and war by Julius Caesar, who thus became "the foremost man of all the world". Napoleon flashes up, meteor like, from the streets of Paris, until he has all the armies of Europe in his train, unable to curb or break his power, because he outmarched, out manoeuvred, and outfought them upon the contested ground. Fortunate, indeed, is he, and we doubt not that such there are, who feels that destiny has chosen him for a certain calling, marked him for a certain work, appointed him to some high task, or led him to the doing of a great deed. But even when destiny seems to be clearly set before us, I hold that it is always conditional. One, to fulfill the destiny he conceives to be appointed to him, must first be properly equipped, both from within and without; he must employ all the means, powers and influences conducive to that end, and he must walk courageously in the path that leads to it.

The possibilities that lie before the youth of America are dazzling to the imagination—limitless. There are no objects of ambition to which he may not aspire, no prize in life for which he may not compete, no path of human endeavor he may not tread, no height of usefulness and honor he may not hope to scale. For here, each one is supposed not only to be entitled to, but to be actually given "a man's chance." Neither rank nor title, wealth nor blood, are supposed to stand as a barrier to the youth of most lowly origin or humble birth. It is our boast, that in America, "each holds his destiny in his own hands". This is, indeed, the very breath of life which this republic was born. It was the spirit of the Pilgrim Fathers when they took their destiny in their hands and set sail for these shores; it was the power that inspired the patriots of the Revolution, when they refused taxation without representation, and launched this nation upon the untried waters of self-government. When opportunity is hedged about by caste, race, or class barriers and distinction, personal responsibility for what an individual may become is not large; but when the pathway of opportunity is made free that all may walk it with unfettered feet, responsibility for individual destiny becomes a sacred trust. Would a young man never be unemployed; let him be thorough in his work and faithful to the interests he serves; would he be prosperous; let him practice rigid economy and honesty; would he be honored by society; let him fulfill his moral, social and civic duties.

Form (from) the time the foundations of the government were laid, America has regarded herself as a nation with a mission. Each epoch in her history has been ascribed to "manifest destiny". America regards herself as a nation raised up by God to establish and preserve certain great principles. It is hers to keep watch and ward over personal freedom, individual liberty, and free self-government established upon no other foundation than manhood citizenship.

Other nations may have their ruling families, but here each family is a ruling family. Others may limit the number of those permitted to participate in the administration of the government; here there is but one qualification, and but one test which applies to all. We give to each individual the opportunity to makes out of himself all, and the very best, he is capable of becoming.

While we make no war upon monarchy or absolutism, we say to the crowned heads of all the earth that we must be left free to work out here upon these shores the great task to which we have dedicated ourselves. Until within the past few years we have worked out the problem in comparative isolation from the rest of the world, we have left to the governments of Europe the questions of the expansion of empire, the subjugation of strange peoples, the exploitation of savage races, and the establishment and government of colonies.

Within the past few years the nation has entered upon the path of a new development. We have acquired territory outside our borders and are now governing strange peoples across thousands of miles of sea on the other side of the world. In this new departure some of the wisest and most patriotic men see the beginning of the republic's end. But, however loudly they may shout their notes of warning, the great mass of the nation is borne forward by the current of events. The step once taken cannot be retraced. In a new sense we have become a world power. But our destiny to continue to be a free self-governing people will not be changed if we do our duty by ourselves and by the peoples with whom we are brought in contact.

While other nations subjugate alien peoples, we must liberate them. While others exploit the material resources of foreign lands, we must develop them. While others force the yoke of their peculiar civilization and government upon unwilling peoples, it is this nation's mission to take them by the hand and assist them in the establishment of a form of government and the development of a civilization suited to their peculiar temperament and climatic conditions.

While within our own borders, with all the commingling of races, the mantle of citizenship must be large enough to enfold them all. When money comes to be more influential than manhood; when color comes to be more potential than the Constitution, then indeed is the axe laid at the roots of our tree of liberty.

Of all the movements of modern times, the social is destined to wield the greatest influence. The social awakening of the people within the last century has brought into organized society a new force. The distant thunder of the tread of marching millions now at last is heard. The America eagle from his mountain height of freedom was the first to see them coming from afar, but now have they drawn so near to courts of justice and thrones of power, that even the Russian bear trembles with alarm at their approach.

The groanings of the social spirit in travail to be born is now often viewed with apprehension. What shall be brought forth, the wisdom of statesmanship cares not now to know. Entrenched wealth says it may be a usurper of its accumulations, while conservatism avers that the time of its delivery is not at hand. But the hour is struck. The hands upon the dial plate of progress cannot be reversed. The process of the readjustment of the relations of men to society has begun, and while many blunders will be made, the work will go on until men have learned to live together upon a new basis, both of interest and of service.

Gone is the time when many shall toil for the benefit and pleasure of the few. Gone is the time when the few shall be surfeited with goods, with houses and lands, while many perish or are but poorly housed and fed. The mass of humanity has grown to look up with aspiration and desire—to all the vast domain of social and industrial advantage from which they have been so long debarred. They will continue to look up, until they rise up, and march in their might as God's children coming into their own.

While these look up, those who are above entrenched in seats of power must look down, not in derision or scorn, not in malice or alarm, but with willingness to surrender to their disinherited brothers the estates they have so long withheld.

The great questions which we and other enlightened nations of the earth are now seeking to solve and settle are being fought, with either segregation or solidarity for their war cry.

For thirty centuries, in the great drama of human civilization, segregation has held the centre of the stage. The line cleavage between man and man, class and class, race and race, nation and nation, has ramified into every phase of human relationship. From of old it has been found that the sun of destiny only shone to light the path of certain privileged classes or races. Men could conceive that certain classes or that a particular race or nation had a destiny worth fighting for; nay, so priceless as to be worthy to be preserved if one must die for it.

That the Jews had a destiny, let even the mountains round about Jerusalem proclaim it. That the Greeks had a destiny, let the marble of Phidias breathe it and the muse of Homer give it voice; that Rome had a destiny, let the Tiber hear the proclamation from her seven hills and bear the message on into the sea; that the white race has a destiny, let the hoarse voice of his cannon thunder it as, robed in blood, he goes forth upon his mission of the subjugation of the world.

At last a new conception is dawning upon mankind and human speech is becoming vaguely articulate, but none the less articulate, in uttering a new word, that word is solidarity. The destiny of the individual, the race, the nation, is becoming less and less, and will have decreasing influence as a rallying cry, only as it includes the common destiny of man. An individual life, a race or national life, which only sees its duty and views its destiny from the angle of these narrow limitations, will become more and more a thing to be despised. The necessity for cooperation among men, their mutual interests and the common good, are bounded by no race or clime. The destiny of our race is bound up with the destiny of the world.

You may call me a dreamer when I tell you that my vision beholds the fetters of race and class broken from the limbs of humanity forever more. I see humanity with arms so long that brother joins hands with other brother across the broad expanse of sea, until, in a circle that girdles the globe, man to his brother man is joined in a loving handclasp around the world.

I see the men of a new civilization rejoicing in the fulfillment of our golden dreams, when from the centuries of its wanderings humanity comes back to its common unity, knowing but one family altar, that the altar of humanity; but one brotherhood, that the brotherhood of man; but one fatherhood, that the fatherhood of God.

◆

Black Theology

National Committee of Black Churchmen, "Black Theology," June 13, 1969. Reprinted from James H. Cone and Gayraud S. Wilmore, editors. *Black Theology: A Documentary History, 1966–1979* (Maryknoll, N.Y.: Orbis, 1979), 100–102 (italics in the original).

Issued during the heated Black Power debate, this document outlines several of the major points that became the heart of black theology. Those involved in the writing of this statement argued for an interpretation of the Christian Gospel in light of the current situation of black Americans. Such a perspective on the Christian faith makes the liberation of black Americans a central concern for God and for those devoted to God. In this sense, theology becomes the articulation of God's commitment to the oppressed.

◆

Black people affirm their being. This affirmation is made in the whole experience of being black in the hostile American society. Black theology is not a gift of the Christian gospel dispensed to slaves; rather it is an *appropriation* that black slaves made of the gospel given by their white oppressors. Black theology has been nurtured, sustained, and passed on in the black churches in their various ways of expression. Black theology has dealt with all the ultimate and violent issues of life and death for a people despised and degraded.

The Black Church has not only nurtured black people but enabled them to survive brutalities that ought not to have been inflicted on any community of men. Black theology is the product of black Christian experience and reflection. It comes out of the past. It is strong in the present. And we believe it is redemptive for the future.

This indigenous theological formation of faith emerged from the stark need of the fragmented black community to affirm itself as a part of the Kingdom of God. White theology sustained the American slave system and negated the humanity of blacks. This indigenous black theology, based on the imaginative black experience, was the best hope for the survival of black people. This is a way of saying that black theology was already present in the spirituals and slave songs and exhortations of slave preachers and their descendants.

All theologies arise out of communal experience with God. At this moment in time, the black community seeks to express its theology in language that speaks to the contemporary mood of black people.

What Is Black Theology?

Black Theology is a theology of black liberation. It seeks to plumb the black condition in the light of God's revelation in Jesus Christ, so that the black community can see that the gospel is commensurate with the achievement of black humanity. Black Theology is a theology of "blackness." It is the affirmation of black humanity that emancipates black people from white racism, thus providing authentic freedom for both white and black people. It affirms the humanity of white people in that it says No to the encroachment of white oppression.

The message of liberation is the revelation of God as revealed in the incarnation of Jesus Christ. Freedom IS the gospel. Jesus is the Liberator! "He . . . hath sent me to preach deliverance to the captives" (Luke 4:18). Thus the black patriarchs and we ourselves know this reality despite all attempts of the white church to obscure it and to utilize Christianity as a means of enslaving blacks. The demand that Christ the Liberator imposes on all men *requires* all blacks to affirm their full dignity as persons and all whites to surrender their presumptions of superiority and abuses of power.

What Does This Mean?

It means that Black Theology must confront the issues which are a part of the reality of black oppression. We cannot ignore the powerlessness of the black community. Despite the *repeated requests* for significant programs of social change, the American people have refused to appropriate adequate sums of money for social reconstruction. White church bodies have often made promises only to follow with default. We must, therefore, once again call the attention of the nation and the church to the need for providing adequate resources of power (reparation). Reparation is a part of the Gospel message. Zaccheus knew well the necessity for repayment as an essential ingredient in repentance. "If I have taken anything from any man by false accusation, I restore him fourfold" (Luke 19:8). The church which calls itself the servant church must, like its Lord, be willing to strip itself of possessions in order to build and restore that which has been destroyed by the compromising bureaucrats and conscienceless rich. While reparation cannot remove the guilt created by the despicable deed of slavery, it is, nonetheless, a positive response to the need for power in the black community. This nation, and, a people who have always related the value of the person to his possession of property, must recognize the necessity of restoring property in order to reconstitute personhood.

What Is the Cost?

Living is risk. We take it in confidence. The black community has been brutalized and victimized over the centuries. The recognition that comes from seeing Jesus as Liberator and the Gospel as freedom empowers black men to risk themselves for freedom and for faith. This faith we affirm in the midst of a hostile, disbelieving society. We intend to exist by this faith at all times and in all places.

In spite of brutal deprivation and denial the black community has appropriated the spurious form of Christianity imposed upon it and made it into an instrument for resisting the extreme demands of oppression. It has enabled the black community to live through unfulfilled promises, unnecessary risks, and inhuman relationships.

As black theologians address themselves to the issues of the black revolution, it is incumbent upon them to say that the black community will not be turned from its course, but will seek complete fulfillment of the promises of the Gospel. Black people have survived the terror. We now commit ourselves to the risks of affirming the dignity of black personhood. We do this as men and as black Christians. This is the message of Black Theology. In the words of Eldridge Cleaver:

We shall have our manhood.

We shall have it or the earth will be leveled by our efforts to gain it.

NOTES

Introduction: The Making of Black Christians

1. Albert Raboteau, *Slave Religion: The "Invisible Institution" in the Antebellum South* (New York: Oxford Univ. Press, 1978), 97.

2. Cotton Mather, "The Negro Christianized: An Essay to Excite and Assist that Good Work, the Instruction of Negro-Servants in Christianity" (Boston, 1706), quoted by Alden T. Vaughan, ed., *The Puritan Tradition in America: 1620–1730* (New York: Harper and Row, 1972), 268.

3. Raboteau, *Slave Religion*, 105–8.

4. Ibid., 104.

5. Ibid., 131.

6. Ibid., 132–33.

7. In years past, discussions concerning the appeal of evangelistic Christianity centered on the question of African cultural retention—the presence of "Africanisms" in American culture. That is to say, it was concerned with the types and strengths of African thought and practice that enslaved Africans incorporated into their New World practices. Some argued that the middle passage was too harsh to allow for significant cultural retention. Others argued that there was evidence of significant retention. It is more commonly held today that there is some significant retention expressed religiously through the style of music, sermons, and expression of religious experience through dance, for example, and less significant practices that draw from an African past.

8. Charles C. Jones, *The Religious Instruction of the Negroes in the United States* (Savannah, Ga., 1842), quoted in Raboteau, 1978, 162–63.

9. Raboteau, *Slave Religion*, 175–76.

10. Michael A. Gomez, *Exchanging Our Country Marks: The Transformation of African Identities in the Colonial and Antebellum South* (Chapel Hill, N.C.: Univ. of North Carolina Press, 1998), 22.

11. For additional information on this perspective see these works by Anthony B. Pinn, *Varieties of African American Religious Experience* (Minneapolis: Fortress Press, 1998), especially chapter 4; *Why, Lord?: Suffering and Evil in Black Theology* (New York: Continuum, 1995); and *By These Hands: A Documentary History of African American Humanism* (New York: New York Univ. Press, forthcoming).

12. "Funny Paper" Smith, "Fool's Blues," in *The Blues Line: A Collection of Blues Lyrics, From Leadbelly to Muddy Waters,* compiled by Eric Sackheim (New York: Ecco Press, 1969), 120.

13. Daniel Alexander Payne, "Daniel Payne's Protestation of Slavery," in *Lutheran Herald and Journal of the Franckean Synod* (August 1, 1839), 114–15.

14. Yvonne P. Chireau, "Hidden Traditions: Black Religion, Magic, and Alternative Spiritual Beliefs in Womanist Perspective," in Jacquelyn Grant, ed., *Perspectives on Womanist Theology*, Black Church Scholars Series 7 (Atlanta: Interdenominational Theological Center Press, 1995), 72.

15. See, for example, Michael A. Gomez, *Exchanging Our Country Marks: The Transformation of African Identities in the Colonial and Antebellum South* (Chapel Hill, N.C.: Univ. of North Carolina Press, 1998); Pinn, *Varieties;* Richard Brent Turner, *Islam in the African-American Experience* (Bloomington, Ind.: Indiana Univ. Press, 1997); George Brandon, *Santeria from Africa to the New World: The Dead Sell Memories* (Bloomington, Ind.: Indiana Univ. Press, 1993); and Joseph E. Holloway, *Africanisms in American Culture* (Bloomington, Ind.: Indiana Univ. Press, 1990).

16. C. Eric Lincoln, *The Black Muslims in America*, 3rd ed. (Grand Rapids, Mich.: Eerdmans, 1994), 257.

17. Frederick Douglass, *Narrative of the Life of Frederick Douglass, an American Slave, Written by Himself* (New York: New American Library, 1968), "Appendix," 120–21.

18. Ira Berlin, Marc Favreau, and Steven F. Miller, editors, *Remembering Slavery: African Americans Talk about Their Personal Experiences of Slavery and Emancipation* (New York: New Press, in association with the Library of Congress, Washington, D. C., 1998), 195–96.

19. Ibid., 205.

20. Levi J. Coppin, *Unwritten History* (1919; rpt. New York: Negro Universities Press, 1968), 245.

21. Jessie Parkhurst Guzman, ed. *Negro Year Book: A Review of Events Affecting Negro Life, 1941–1946* (Tuskegee, Ala.: Department of Records and Research of the Tuskegee Institute, 1946).

22. Joseph Washington, "How Black Is Black Religion?" in James J. Gardiner, and J. Deotis Roberts, eds., *Quest for a Black Theology* (Philadelphia: Pilgrim Press, 1971), 28.

23. This volume is supplemented by Anthony Pinn's *Black Church Activism in the Post–Civil Rights Era* (Orbis, forthcoming), which gives primary attention to the Black Church's work from 1970 to the present. As a note on terminology, readers will quickly recognize that we use the terms "Black" and "African American" interchangeably. Also, we typically refer to enslaved Africans as "Africans," and we usually limit the term "African American" to post–Civil War references.

24. The following sources were consulted in the completion of these bibliographies: Bettye Collier-Thomas, *Daughters of Thunder: Black Women Preachers and Their Sermons, 1850–1979* (San Francisco: Jossey-Bass, 1998); Larry G. Murphy, J. Gordon Melton, and Gary L. Ward, eds., *Encyclopedia*

of African American Religions (New York: Garland, 1993); Judith Weisenfeld and Richard Newman, *This Far by Faith: Readings in African-American Women's Religious Biography* (New York: Routledge, 1996).

1. African American Methodist Churches

1. Anthony Armstrong, *The Church of England, the Methodists and Society, 1700–1850* (Totowa, N.J.: Rowman and Littlefield, 1973), 63–65.

2. Leslie F. Church, *The Early Methodist People* (New York: Philosophical Library, 1949), 98–99.

3. Henry Abelove, *The Evangelist of Desire: John Wesley and the Methodists* (Stanford: Stanford Univ. Press, 1990), 5; William R. Cannon, "Accomplishments to Wesley's Death," in William K. Anderson, ed., *Methodism* (New York: Methodist Publishing House, 1957), 37.

4. Frank Baker, *From Wesley to Asbury: Studies in Early American Methodism* (Durham: Duke Univ. Press, 1976), 29–30.

5. William Warren Sweet, *The Rise of Methodism in the West, Being the Journal of the Western Conference, 1800–1811* (New York: Methodist Book Concern; reprint, Nashville: Smith & Lamar, 1920), 15.

6. Cynthia L. Lyerly, *Methodism and the Southern Mind, 1770–1810* (New York: Oxford Univ. Press, 1998), 151.

7. Dwight W. Culver, *Negro Segregation in the Methodist Church* (New Haven: Yale Univ. Press, 1953), 42.

8. Francis Asbury, *Journal*, vol. 3, "February 11, 1797," 160.

9. Raboteau, *Slave Religion*, 131, 175; Lyerly, *Methodism*, appendix, 187; Culver, *Negro Segregation*, 50.

10. John Dixon Long, *Pictures of Slavery in Church and State* (1857; reprint, New York: Negro Universities Press, 1969), 157–58, 159.

11. Raboteau, *Slave Religion*, 226.

12. Lyerly, *Methodism*, 52.

13. Long, *Pictures of Slavery*, 27–28.

14. Donald G. Mathews, *Slavery and Methodism: A Chapter in American Morality, 1780–1845* (Princeton, N.J.: Princeton Univ. Press, 1965), 13.

15. Quoted in Harry V. Richardson. *Dark Salvation: The Story of Methodism as It Developed among Blacks in America* (Garden City, N.Y.: Doubleday, 1976), 72.

16. James T. Campbell, *Songs of Zion: The African Methodist Episcopal Church in the United States and South Africa* (New York: Oxford Univ. Press, 1995), 10; Carol R. V. George, *Segregated Sabbaths: Richard Allen and the Emergence of Independent Black Churches, 1760–1840* (New York: Oxford Univ. Press, 1973), 45; Richard Allen, "Journal of Richard Allen," in Daniel A. Payne, *History of the African Methodist Episcopal Church* (New York: Arno

Press, 1969), 82. Also found in Howard D. Gregg, *History of the African Methodist Episcopal Church: The Black Church in Action* (Nashville: AMEC Sunday School Union, 1980), 16–24.

17. Payne, *History,* 14.

18. Ibid., 85–87.

19. Campbell, *Songs of Zion,* 34.

20. Jarena Lee, "The Life and Religious Experience of Jarena Lee," in William L. Andrews, ed., *Sisters of the Spirit: Three Black Women's Autobiographies of the Nineteenth Century* (Bloomington: Indiana Univ. Press, 1986), 36.

21. Ibid.

22. Richardson, *Dark Salvation,* 196.

23. Henry McNeal Turner, "The American Colonization Society," *African Repository* 51:2 (April 1875), rpt. in Edwin S. Redkey, ed., *Respect Black: The Writings and Speeches of Henry McNeal Turner* (New York: Arno Press, 1971), 42.

24. William J. Walls, *The African Methodist Episcopal Zion Church: Reality of the Black Church* (Charlotte, N.C.: AME Zion Publishing House, 1974), 51; Christopher Rush, "Rise of the African Methodist Episcopal Zion Church," in Milton Sernett, ed., *Afro-American Religious History: A Documentary Witness* (Durham: Duke Univ. Press, 1985), 151.

25. Walls, *African Methodist Episcopal Zion Church,* 27.

26. Richardson, *Dark Salvation,* 120–26.

27. Walls, *African Methodist Episcopal Church,* 84–90.

28. Richardson, *Dark Salvation,* 137.

29. Andrews, *Sisters in the Spirit,* 202.

30. Ibid., 209.

31. Calvin Marshall III, "The Black Church: Its Mission Is Liberation," in C. Eric Lincoln, *The Black Experience in Religion* (Garden City, N.Y.: Anchor Press, 1974), 159.

32. Walls, *African Methodist Episcopal Church,* 252.

33. Ibid., 541–42.

34. Richardson, *Dark Salvation,* 227.

35. Ibid.

36. Lucius H. Holsey, "The Colored Methodist Episcopal Church," in Sernett, *Afro-American Religious History*, 238.

37. William E. Montgomery, *Under Their Own Vine and Fig Tree: The African-American Church in the South, 1865–1900* (Baton Rouge, La.: Louisiana State Univ. Press, 123.

38. Isaac Lane, "From Slave to Preacher Among the Freedmen," in Sernett, *Afro-American Religious History*, 233.

39. Holsey, "The Colored Methodist Episcopal Church," in Sernett, *Afro-American Religious History*, 237.

40. Ibid.

2. African American Baptist Churches

1. Quoted in W. Clark Gilpin, *The Millenarian Piety of Roger Williams* (Chicago: The Univ. of Chicago Press, 1979), 50.

2. James Melvin Washington, *Frustrated Fellowship: The Black Baptist Quest for Social Power* (Macon, Ga.: Mercer Univ. Press, 1986), 4–5.

3. Sydney E. Ahlstrom, *A Religious History of the American People* (New Haven: Yale Univ. Press, 1972), 172.

4. Gilpin, *Millenarian Piety,* 30–32.

5. David S. Lovejoy, *Religious Enthusiasm in the New World: Heresy to Revolution* (Cambridge: Harvard Univ. Press, 1985), 59–60.

6. Ahlstrom, *Religious History,* 171.

7. Ibid.

8. Mechal Sobel, *Trabelin' On: The Slave Journey to an Afro-Baptist Faith* (Westport, Conn.: Greenwood, 1979), 85.

9. Ibid., 84.

10. Ibid., 88.

11. Ibid., 169.

12. Ira Berlin, Marc Favreau, and Steven F. Miller, eds., *Remembering Slavery: African Americans Talk about Their Personal Experience of Slavery and Emancipation* (New York: New Press, 1998), 276–77.

13. Quoted in Sobel, *Trabelin' On,* 1979, 105.

14. C. Eric Lincoln and Lawrence Mamiya, *The Black Church in the African American Experience* (Durham: Duke Univ. Press, 1990), 23–24.

15. James M. Simms, *The First Colored Baptist Church in North America* (Philadelphia: J. B. Lippincott Co., 1888; reprint. New York: Negro Universities Press, 1969), 19–20.

16. Paul Harvey, *Redeeming the South: Religious Cultures and Racial Identities among Southern Baptists, 1865–1925* (Chapel Hill: Univ. of North Carolina Press, 1997), 49.

17. Gayraud Wilmore, *Black Religion and Black Radicalism: An Interpretation of the Religious History of Afro-American People,* 2nd ed. (Maryknoll, N.Y.: Orbis, 1983), 68.

18. Nathaniel Paul, "African Baptists Celebrate Emancipation in New York State," in Sernett, ed., *Afro-American Religious History,* 182.

19. The terms "association" and "convention" had flexible usage during these early years. However, association was often used to denote clusters of churches that extended beyond a few local churches but did not necessarily cover more than a portion of a state or an entire state. Convention, at times, was the reference for a unit smaller than an association, but with time it came to connote a collective of Baptist churches extending beyond the jurisdiction of any one association in that it contained a number of these units.

20. Statistical information in this section of chapter 2 are drawn from these sources: James Washington's *Frustrated Fellowship* (Mercer Univ. Press, 1986); Albert Raboteau's *Slave Religion: The Invisible Institution in the Antebellum South* (New York: Oxford Univ. Press, 1978); Leroy Fitts, *A History of Black Baptists* (Nashville: Broadman, 1985); Margaret Washington Creel, *"A Peculiar People": Slave Religion and Community-Culture among the Gullahs* (New York: New York Univ. Press, 1988); Sobel, *Trabelin' On*; Will B. Gravely, "The Rise of African Churches in America, 1786–1822," in Timothy Fulop and Albert Raboteau, *African American Religion: Interpretive Essays in History and Culture* (New York: Routledge, 1997).

21. Quoted in James Washington, *Frustrated Fellowship*, 34.

22. Harvey, *Redeeming the South,* 63.

23. Evelyn Brooks Higginbotham, *Righteous Discontent: The Women's Movement in the Black Baptist Church, 1880–1920* (Cambridge: Harvard Univ. Press, 1993), 5–8.

24. Harvey, *Redeeming the South,* 73.

25. Quoted in Fitts, *History of Black Baptists,* 89.

26. Harvey, *Redeeming the South,* 229.

27. Higginbotham, *Righteous Discontent,* 121.

28. Nannie Helen Burroughs, "Not Color but Character," in Marcia Y. Riggs, ed., *Can I Get a Witness?: Prophetic Religious Voices of African American Women, an Anthology* (Maryknoll, N.Y.: Orbis, 1997), 87.

29. Harvey, *Redeeming the South,* 243–44.

30. Ibid., 245.

31. Sernett, *Bound for the Promised Land,* 98.

32. Ibid.

33. We recognize that this timeline is not as extensive as the others, but efforts to obtain additional information directly from the National Baptist Convention of America's headquarters failed.

34. Sernett, *Bound for the Promised Land,* 111.

35. There was a schism within this convention resulting in the formation of the National Missionary Baptist Convention of America (1988).

36. Joseph H. Jackson, *A Story of Christian Activism: The History of the National Baptist Convention, U.S.A., Inc.* (Nashville: Townsend Press, 1980), 269.

37. Ibid., 276.

38. In 1984 the convention limited the president's time in office to ten years.

39. Jackson, *Story of Christian Activism,* 486.

40. Fitts, *Black Baptists,* 103–4.

41. See the church's website, www.pnbc.org/frameindex.htm, in the section called "National News Release and Call Letter from 1961."

42. See the church's website, www.pnbc.org/frameindex.htm, in the section called "The Progressive Concept."

3. African American Pentecostalism

1. Two perspectives dominate discussions concerning the development of the Holiness and Pentecostal movements in the United States: (1) the sanctification and indwelling of the Holy Spirit represent a particular take on the religious fervor and growth associated with the Great Awakenings; (2) the sanctification doctrine represents a unique, third phase of development beyond the Great Awakenings and the Holiness movement—marked by reform extending beyond earlier attempts at spiritual renewal. There has been a debate over the origins of the Pentecostal movement. Are African Americans responsible for its start or was it an interracial endeavor? We tend to give more attention to African American involvement beginning with William Seymour. However, examination of this debate is beyond the scope of this volume. For concise information on it see Iain MacRobert, *The Black Roots and White Racism of Early Pentecostalism in the USA* (New York: St. Martin's Press, 1988), chapter 7. Whichever perspective one holds, it remains clear that personal salvation and its evidence encompassed the spiritual aspirations of groups that cut across racial, gender, and class lines.

2. Stated in Cheryl J. Sanders, *Saints in Exile: The Holiness-Pentecostal Experience in African American Religion and Culture* (New York: Oxford Univ. Press, 1996), 15.

3. Vinson Synan, *The Holiness-Pentecostal Tradition: Charismatic Movements in the Twentieth Century* (Grand Rapids, Mich.: Eerdmans, 1997), 23.

4. Ibid., 25.

5. Quoted in Judith Weisenfeld and Richard Newman, eds., *This Far by Faith: Readings in African-American Women's Religious Biography* (New York: Routledge, 1996), 6.

6. Levi Coppin, "The Negro's Part in the Redemption of Africa," in Stephen Angell and Anthony B. Pinn, eds., *Social Protest Thought in the African Methodist Episcopal Church, 1862–1939* (Knoxville: Univ. of Tennessee Press, 2000), 220.

7. Synan, *Holiness-Pentecostal Tradition,* 39–43.

8. Acts of the Apostles 2:1-4, *The Living Bible* (paraphrased)

9. MacRobert, *Black Roots,* 37.

10. There is a third group not discussed here. Those within this third group are referred to as holders of the Apostolic faith, which is definable in light of two essential elements: speaking in tongues as the only evidence of the Holy Spirit's presence and baptism of adults in the name of Jesus only.

11. MacRobert, *Black Roots,* 43–44.

12. Ibid., 46.

13. Synan, *Holiness-Pentecostal Tradition,* 92.

14. Ibid., 93.

15. MacRobert, *Black Roots,* 53.

16. From the *Apostolic Faith* newspaper published by Seymour's group, quoted in MacRobert, *Black Roots,* 5.

17. MacRobert, *Black Roots,* 35.

18. Elsie W. Mason, "Bishop C. H. Mason, Church of God in Christ," in Sernett, ed. *Afro-American Religious History,* 286.

19. Ibid., 287.

20. Ibid., 289.

21. Ibid., 293.

22. Other gifts of the spirit include prophesy, interpretation of tongues, teaching, preaching and healing.

23. Sanders, *Saints in Exile,* 31.

24. According to all accounts, COGIC was the only incorporated denomination of the Pentecostal faith. All those interested in ordination and other activities requiring church authority, whether black or white, had to go through COGIC. White ministers were content to be ordained by Mason and, at least in a limited sense, associate with the denomination until 1914 when race bias resulted in the formation of the all-white Assemblies of God denomination.

25. Church of God in Christ official website: http://www.cogic.org/hist.htm.

4. Liberation Thought and the Black Church

1. Carol V. R. George, *Segregated Sabbaths: Richard Allen and the Rise of Independent Black Churches, 1760–1840* (New York: Oxford Univ. Press, 1973), 117, 122.

2. James Washington, *Frustrated Fellowship: The Black Baptist Quest for Social Power* (Macon, Ga.: Mercer Univ. Press, 1986), 8.

3. Iain MacRobert, *The Black Roots and White Racism of Early Pentecostalism in the USA* (New York: St. Martin's, 1988), 34.

4. Reverdy C. Ransom, "The Institutional Church," in Anthony B. Pinn, ed., *Making the Gospel Plain: The Writings of Bishop Reverdy C. Ransom* (Harrisburg, Pa.: Trinity Press International, 1999), 198.

5. Ida B. Wells-Barnett, "Lynching, Our National Crime," in Marcia Y. Riggs, ed., *Can I Get a Witness? Prophetic Religious Voices of African American Women: An Anthology* (Maryknoll, N.Y.: Orbis, 1997), 150.

6. Phyl Garland, "I Remember Adam: TV Documentary Revives Interest in Rev. Adam Clayton Powell Jr.," *Ebony,* March 1990, 56, 58.

7. Quoted in Charles V. Hamilton, *Adam Clayton Powell, Jr.: The Political Biography of an American Dilemma* (New York: Collier, 1992), 86.

8. Ella Josephine Baker, "Roots," in *Can I Get a Witness?,* 164.

9. Fannie Lou Hamer, "Sick and Tired of Being Sick and Tired," in *Can I Get a Witness?,* 179–80.

10. Bernice Johnson Reagon, "Women as Culture Carriers in the Civil Rights Movement: Fannie Lou Hamer," in Vicki L. Crawford, et al., *Women*

in the Civil Rights Movement: Trailblazers and Torchbearers, 1941–1965 (Brooklyn, N.Y.: Carlson, 1990), 211.

11. Clayborne Carson, ed., *The Autobiography of Martin Luther King, Jr.* (New York: Warner, 1998), 200–201.

12. National Committee of Negro Churchmen, "Racism and the Elections: The American Dilemma, 1966," in James H. Cone and Gayraud Wilmore, *Black Theology: A Documentary History, 1966–1979* (Maryknoll, N.Y.: Orbis, 1979), 31.

13. National Committee of Negro Churchmen, "Black Power," in ibid., 23.

14. A copy of this document and other relevant early materials is available in Cone and Wilmore, eds., *Black Theology*.

15. "The Black Manifesto," in ibid., 83–84.

16. "The National Committee of Black Churchmen's Response to the Black Manifesto," in ibid., 90–92.

17. "Statement by the National Committee of Black Churchmen, June 13, 1969," in ibid., 100–101, 1.

18. James H. Cone, *A Black Theology of Liberation*, 20th anniv. ed. (Maryknoll, N.Y.: Orbis, 1986), 23.

19. This assertion countered Joseph Washington's argument that the Black Church was irrelevant. He would later soften his position. See Washington, *Black Religion: The Negro and Christianity in the United States* (Boston: Beacon, 1964); and Washington, *The Politics of God* (Boston: Beacon, 1967).

20. James H. Cone, *My Soul Looks Back* (Nashville: Abingdon, 1982); James Cone, *Black Theology and Black Power* (New York: Seabury, 1969). The quotation is from the "Preface to the 1989 Edition" of *Black Theology and Black Power*, 20th anniv. ed. (San Francisco: Harper & Row, 1989), vii. For an important exploration of the public dimensions of Cone's first books see Dwight Hopkins, ed., *Black Faith and Public Talk: Critical Essays on James H. Cone's Black Theology and Black Power* (Maryknoll, N.Y.: Orbis, 1999). Also see the companion essays by Delores Williams, Gayraud Wilmore, and others in the anniversary edition of Cone's *A Black Theology of Liberation*.

21. Cone, *A Black Theology of Liberation*, 63.

22. James H. Harris, "Black Church and Black Theology: Theory and Practice," in James H. Cone and Gayraud S. Wilmore, eds., *Black Theology: A Documentary History, 1980–1992*, vol. 2 (Maryknoll, N.Y.: Orbis, 1993), 86.

23. Gayraud Wilmore, "Introduction," in ibid., 79.

24. Dwight N. Hopkins, "Black Theology and a Second Generation: New Scholarship and New Challenges," in ibid., 68.

25. Frances Beale, "Double Jeopardy: To Be Black and Female," in Cone and Wilmore, eds., *Black Theology*, vol. 1, 370.

26. Ibid., 376.

27. James H. Cone, *For My People: Black Theology and the Black Church* (Maryknoll, N.Y.: Orbis Books, 1984), 101.

GLOSSARY

Abolition movement: The movement to end slavery in the United States.

Africanism: A term commonly used as a reference to the retention of African culture within the cultural production of black Americans.

altar call: The time during which members of the congregation are invited to come to the altar for prayer.

Antebellum Period: American history prior to the Civil War.

association: A collection of local Baptist churches on a regional level, usual associated with particular cities or states.

atheism: Disbelief in the existence of God.

baptism: An event after conversion during which a new convert goes through a symbolic rebirth. Black denominations debate whether the person needs to be submerged in water or if sprinkling with water will have the same effect. Others argue over whether baptism must take place in the name of Jesus or if the entire Trinity must be invoked.

baptism in the Holy Spirit: The process of being filled with the Holy Spirit. This can occur only after a person has accepted Jesus Christ as personal savior.

Bible study: A special church activity during which members of a church receive instruction in biblical teachings.

bishop: Highest ranking minister within the black Methodist churches. Also a high ranking figure in the Church of God in Christ.

Black Church: Term used to denote the collective presence of various black denominations.

black liberation theology: Also called black theology, this is a form of theology developed in the late 1960s that gives priority to social transformation as the primary concern of the Christian Gospel.

"Black Manifesto": A declaration made during the 1960s at Riverside Church in New York that sparked an interest in Black Power on the part of many black ministers.

Black Power: Term used in the 1960s to connote strong black consciousness and the end of racism's sociopolitical and economic connotations.

Book of Discipline: The manual containing the basic doctrine and regulations of a denomination.

camp meeting: An energetic worship service held outside a traditional church edifice.

catechism: Basic elements of the faith taught in a question and answer format.

charismatic: Style of religious expression marked by energetic involvement in services.

Civil Rights movement: The collective struggle for social transformation of African American rights during the late 1950s through the late 1960s. The Black Church played a prominent role in this movement.

conference: A collection of local Methodist churches based on geographic areas.

congregation: Collection of like-minded Christian under the leadership of a minister.

connectional church: A reference to all the local churches that make up a particular denomination.

convention: Interstate collections of Baptist churches, usually national in scope.

conversion: The acceptance of Jesus Christ as one's personal savior—often referred to as being "born again."

Curse of Ham: Reference to the Genesis story of Noah's son, Ham, who is supposedly cursed because he sees his father naked. It is, however, Ham's son Canaan who is cursed. This story was historically used to justify the enslavement of Africans because it was argued that Africans were the descendants of Ham.

dancing in the spirit: The energetic bodily movements displayed by persons possessed by the Holy Spirit.

deacon: The first level of ordained ministry in the black Methodist churches.

deaconness: A position within the Black Church developed for women and having responsibilities for much of the church's outreach activities.

denomination: A collection of churches based upon an accepted body of beliefs and practices.

deradicalization: The term used by historian Gayraud Wilmore to describe the Black Church's turn toward otherworldliness during the Great Migration.

divine calling: The recognition by an individual that he or she has been selected by God to be a minister.

doctrine: Basic beliefs of a denomination.

elder: The second level of ordained ministry in the black Methodist churches.

evangelize: The spreading of the Christian message.

faith: The acceptance of expected events based on belief in God and the benefits of this belief.

general assembly: The division of the Church of God in Christ's internal structure responsible for doctrine and legislation.

general board: Governing body within the Church of God in Christ when the general assembly is not in session.

general conference: The major national meeting within black Methodist denominations.

gifts of the spirit: Phrase used to describe the talents and abilities given to those who have accepted Jesus Christ as their personal Savior and have the indwelling of the Holy Spirit.

glossolalia: Speaking in tongues (or with new tongues) associated with possession by the Holy Spirit.

gradualism: An approach to social transformation that understands progress as a slow process taking place in various stages.

Great Awakenings: The two periods, one during the mid-eighteenth century and the other during the early nineteenth century, when revivals spread across the country and large numbers joined churches.

holiness: The quest for purification, or sanctification, through proper relationship with God and removal of worldly distractions.

holy dance: Also referred to as dancing in the spirit, it entails the bodily movement of Christians during possession by the Holy Ghost or Holy Spirit.

Holy Ghost: Third person of the Trinity that, according to many black Christians, provides spiritual power and authority.

hush harbor meeting: A secret religious meeting held by slaves.

invisible institution: A reference to slave religious activities and community prior to the Civil War.

laity: Reference to nonministerial members of a church.

love feast: The services prior to communion during which participants share water and bread. The purpose is to prepare oneself for communion through fellowship with other Christians.

missionary: Nonordained church worker responsible for take the Gospel of Christ to various communities.

National Conference of Black Churchmen (NCBC): Organization developed in the 1960s to give black clergy a forum for responding to the Black Power movement.

otherworldliness: The term used to describe a church's preoccupation with spiritual growth over socioeconomic and political transformation.

Pentecostals: Those who believe that the indwelling of the Holy Spirit is attested to through speaking in tongues.

polity: Rules and regulation for denominational conduct.

praxis: The thoughtful and informed activity that Christians participate in as they seek social transformation.

prayer: Communication between the believer and God.

prayer bands: Groups of Christians joined together for the purpose of prayer and fellowship.

prayer meeting: A weekly church service devoted to testimonies and prayer.

presiding elder: The church leader responsible for supervising a particular region within the bishop's larger episcopal district.

Protestant: A term derived from those who "protested" against sixteenth-century religious authority. A member of one of the Christian communities resulting from this initial protest. Most black Christians are Protestants.

ontological blackness: Usually a reference to God's deep connection with oppressed black people that results in God's very being (or essence) being associated with the blackness of this oppressed people. With respect to Christians in general it is a reference to the strong commitment to the oppressed that should mark the activities of the church.

religion: Systematized beliefs, doctrines, rituals, and practices usually expressed within a community of like-minded people.

revival: A special and energetic service (or series of services) with the primary focus on converting sinners.

righteousness: Associated with being in proper relationship with God.

ring shout: A practice originating during the period of slavery when believers formed a circle and moved while praying and singing.

sacred: A reference to the realm of life marked by God's presence, or the holy in more general terms.

sanctification: The step beyond salvation, through the grace of God, by which the Christian is set aside for holiness and the exercise of God's will.

schisms: A reference to splits within a religious community over disagreements with respect to doctrine, church leadership, etc.

shouting: Energetic response to the Holy Spirit.

social gospel: A reference to social Christianity and the belief that the Christian faith has ramifications for daily living and consequences that should inspire believers to seek social transformation.

Society for the Propagation of the Gospel in Foreign Parts: The Anglican based organization that began a rather limited attempt to convert slaves in the early 1700s.

Southern Christian Leadership Conference: Organization developed during the Civil Rights movement to coordinate the Black Church's involvement.

steward: A position within various black denominations responsible for certain elements of the church's spiritual concerns.

stewardess: An office within the Black Church for women that is primarily concerned with maintaining the items and spaces necessary for ritual activity.

trial sermon: The first sermon preached by an individual who claims to have a divine calling to ministry.

trustee: A position within various black denominations responsible for the maintenance of the church's physical plant.

Women's Club movement: The unified activities of Black Church women to uplift the black community and secure full rights for women.

worship: The expression of communal or individual devotion to God.

INDEX

◆———————————————◆

Abernathy, Ralph D., 96
Abyssinian Baptist Church in New
    York City, 72
Acts of the Apostles, 106, 112
African American Baptist church
    collectives
    importance of, 72–73
    racial issues and, 75
    sectional interests of, 75
African American Baptist churches,
    63–101
abolition and, 72, 73
autonomy of, 75
    Civil War, Reconstruction and,
        74–75
    conventions of, 73–74
    first congregations of, 68–69
    missionary work of, 73
    nineteenth century expansion of,
        69–70
    pre-Civil War growth, 72
    regional collectives and, 72–73
    social concerns and, 70
African American Baptists, 68
    North-South discussion, 71
    slavery and, 71
    white Baptists and, 71, 75
African American Christians, 77
African American churches
    institutional churches and, 127–28
African American communities
    power dynamics and, 138-39
African American Methodists, 79
African American Pentecostalism,
    102–21, 111
African Americans
    rejection of gospel justifying
        slavery by, 11–12
    religious conversion of, 1–4
African Baptists. *See* African Ameri-
    can Baptists
African Methodist Episcopal (AME)
    Church, 10, 31–42, 127, 149
    annual conferences of, 34

Brown, Morris and, 40
changing nature of African
    American community and, 39
Civil War, Reconstruction and,
    37–38, 42
denouncement of racism from, 38
development of, 31–40, 40
discrimination and limitations for
    women in, 37
educational emphasis of, 35
Evans, Mary G. and, 41
growth of, 34–35, 37
leaders of, 40–42
Lee, Jarena and, 41
missionary activity of, 35, 37–38
modern day infrastructure of,
    39–40
nationalism of, 38
Ransom, Reverdy C. and, 41–42
salvation for blacks by, 37–38
South Carolina Conference of, 37
timeline of, 34
Turner, Henry McNeal and, 42
women and, 35–37, 40
African Methodist Episcopal Church
    in America, 45
African Methodist Episcopal Church
    of New York City, 51
*African Methodist Episcopal Church
    Review,* 35, 42, 48
African Methodist Episcopal Zion
    (AME Zion) Church, 44–53, 127,
    135
    Book Concern and, 53
    Civil Rights movement and, 51
    Clinton, Joseph Jackson and, 52
    development of, 51
    early twentieth century social
        agenda of, 50–51
    education and, 48
    foreign missions of, 48
    "freedom church" and, 50
    growth of, 47–48
    leaders of, 52–53